Old Langford

An Illustrated History, 1850 to 1950

Maureen Duffus

Lisa Francis, Research Assistant

National Library of Canada Cataloguing in Publication

Duffus, Maureen
    Old Langford : an illustrated history, 1850 to 1950 / Maureen Duffus.

Includes bibliographical references and index.
ISBN 0-9733809-0-X

    1. Langford (B.C.)—History. 2. Langford (B.C.)—Biography.
I. Title.

FC3845.L348D8 2003   971.1'28   C2003-905450-0

The publisher acknowledges with thanks, a donation of $1000 from the District of Langford, provided from the Mayor's Charity Golf Tournament.

Cover photo, maps and book design by Jim Bisakowski, Desktop Publishing Ltd., Victoria
    desktoppublishing@shaw.ca   www.bookpublishingservices.com

Published by Town and Gown Press, 9 Price Road, Victoria, B.C.
westnews@shaw.ca

Printed and bound in Canada

Contents

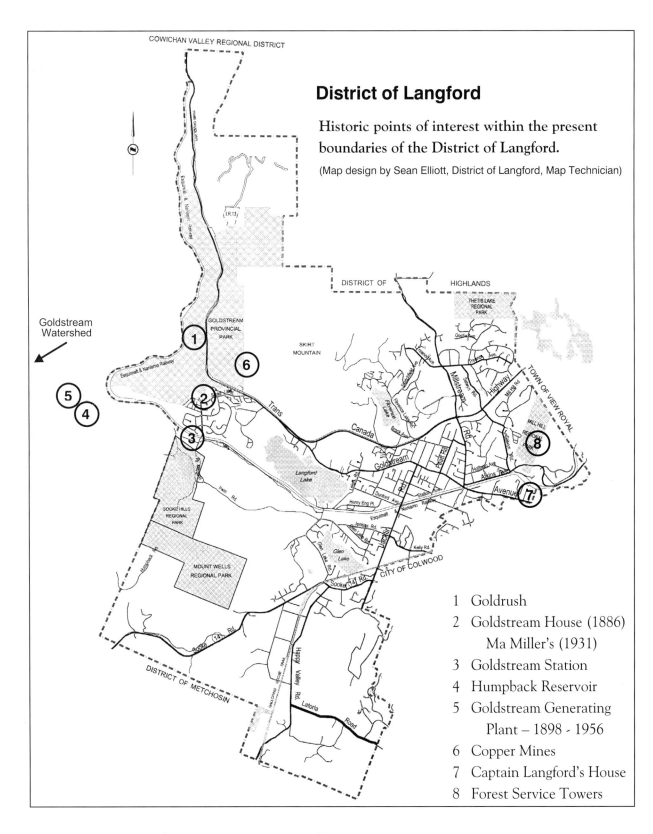

District of Langford

Historic points of interest within the present boundaries of the District of Langford.

(Map design by Sean Elliott, District of Langford, Map Technician)

1 Goldrush
2 Goldstream House (1886)
  Ma Miller's (1931)
3 Goldstream Station
4 Humpback Reservoir
5 Goldstream Generating
  Plant – 1898 - 1956
6 Copper Mines
7 Captain Langford's House
8 Forest Service Towers

Preface

As Langford moves forward to prominence in the region we should not forget its rich historical background. This book brings together for the first time the story of the early years of the Hudson's Bay Company's large farm, the mini-goldrush at Goldstream, the area's popularity with 19th century picnickers, hunters and fishermen all the way through to the beginnings of the rural village and the immigration of settlers between the two world wars.

This well-illustrated history with archival photographs as well as faded snapshots lent by pioneer families gives the flavour of old Langford, the foundation for the thriving municipality of today with its beautifully landscaped pedestrian core, thriving business areas, lavish parks and trails and comfortable new neighbourhoods.

Stewart Young
Mayor of Langford

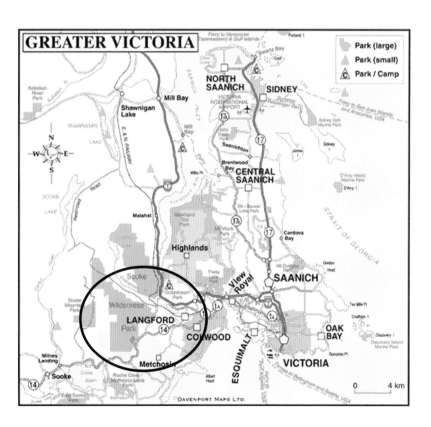

Introduction

This book is the story of early communities within the District of Langford, and of some of the families whose records go back to the 19th century. It is also a story of Langford's sadly neglected early history from the days when Vancouver Island first became a British Colony.

Current maps of the southern tip of Vancouver Island show Victoria, the capital of British Columbia, surrounded by satellite towns, municipalities and districts. Thanks to separatist political decisions of the 1980s and '90s there are 12 of these along the ocean shores between Sidney and Sooke – and one without a coastline. That's Langford. Its access to salt water is confined to the estuary of the Goldstream River as it flows into Finlayson Arm.

However, Langford does have small scenic lakes, fair-sized mountains, gravelly soil left by ancient glaciers, and a history unique amongst its neighbours. It is the only one with a real gold rush in its colourful past.

A history of Langford would be incomplete without reference to the Hudson's Bay Company's half-hearted attempts to colonize southern Vancouver Island in the 1850s. Early European settlement in the heavily forested area west of Fort Victoria, known as the Esquimalt District, began when Captain Edward Edwards Langford arrived to manage a 600 acre Company farm. It was part of the land purchased from Coast Salish Indian families in 1850 by Chief Factor James Douglas, following instructions from Hudson's Bay Company headquarters in London.

The Esquimalt farm, or Colwood Farm as it was named by Captain Langford, extended from Paterson Point at the west end of Esquimalt Harbour in a narrow tract running inland to the land that is now the Royal Colwood Golf Club.

Captain Langford and his family spent a tumultuous decade in the Colony, from their arrival in May 1851, to their forced departure in 1861. He was there when 'hoards' of miners tramped across the Langford Plains to Goldstream, hoping that this conveniently located strike would prove as spectacular as the Fraser River gold rush of 1858-60. It didn't, but the beautiful Goldstream country has attracted visitors ever since.

The next influx of visitors came in the late 1880s on the Esquimalt and Nanaimo Railway. Day trippers came from town on the excursion trains (25 cent fare) to enjoy band concerts and picnics at the popular Goldstream House resort hotel. The Esquimalt Water Works, begun at Goldstream in 1890 as the first part of the present Greater Victoria Water District, and British Columbia's first hydro electric generating plant, built in 1898, brought a slight increase in population at the turn of the century.

Victoria became a city in 1861, but Langford had no part in the city's steady growth for the rest of the century. Hard working farm families, some of whom had immigrated as workers for the HBC farms, acquired land and did the best they could with it. Other early pioneer families began farming between 1870 and the 1890s. Later settlers, including veterans of the Boer War and World War I, came to Langford in the early 20th century.

Interviews with descendants of these families have been a major source of information for the second section of the book. Their stories and photographs have helped greatly to recreate the look and feel of the rural communities before World War II.

Since December, 1992, Langford has elected its own mayor and council and is fervently independent, as are its close neighbours: rural Metchosin, developmentally-inclined Colwood, the anti-development Highlands, and the Town of View Royal through which all Langfordians pass on their way to and from Victoria. There are persistent calls for amalgamation of the satellite towns, followed by cries of horror at the idea of forcing pro and anti-development jurisdictions to unite. So far, the collective will of the people from the west inclines toward separatism and independence, but this history of an earlier Langford inevitably ventures across present day borders to include pertinent stories from the neighbours.

The stories have been checked whenever possible, but recollections differ. Some, like the claim that World War II pilots did practice bombing runs by dropping flour sacks on the straight stretch of railway tracks alongside Station Avenue, seem outrageous. But then a lot of interesting things happened in days gone by. Can anyone confirm this one?

SECTION 1

19TH CENTURY LANGFORD

Langford, 1850 – a first impression from Dr. Helmcken

" … *The Captain [Wishart] and I used to walk about what is now called the Langford Plains and thereabouts … It was an awfully pretty place, covered with grass and wild flowers, and red-winged starlings flitted about in the willows – there were no trails in the bush then but the bush and forest have much grown up there since.*" *Fort Victoria doctor John Sebastian Helmcken's 1890 reminiscences, describing his arrival on the first voyage of the Norman Morison in 1850. Fort Victoria was established in 1843.*

The young town of Victoria as Captain Langford would have seen it after the Fraser River gold rush. brought thousands of miner's to the Hudson's Bay fur trade headquarters. This engraving from the Illustrated London News of 1863 shows Yates Street looking west toward Wharf Street, with an open drain and some tree stumps remaining in front of the new Bank of British Columbia. (From author's copy of original newspaper clipping)

1

CAPTAIN LANGFORD'S TURBULENT YEARS

" ... I have great confidence that his farm, which really is a credit to the Colony, will now make a considerable return for the outlay." James Douglas in support of Captain Langford, 1855.

" ... Mr. Langford is a person wholly unworthy of credence ... singularly deficient in judgment, temper and discretion ..." Douglas to the Duke of Newcastle, British Colonial Secretary, 1863.

The controversial Captain Edward Edwards Langford, a later portrait of the bailiff, or manager, of the Puget Sound Agricultural Company's farm he called Colwood. (BC Archives F-09874)

Captain Edward Edwards Langford was one of the notable figures at Fort Victoria during the 1850s. The former officer in the British Army's 73rd Regiment decided in 1850 to emigrate to a new Pacific island colony as bailiff, or manager, of a large Hudson's Bay Company farm. He and his family lived in style at the farm he called Colwood until he was forced to leave in disgrace in 1860.

Why the 41-year old military gentleman chose to leave England is not known. Unexplained financial difficulties are thought to be the most likely reason. A gentleman farmer in Sussex without independent income, as Langford appears to have been, would need a decently large income to support his wife Flora and their five daughters in the style expected of the officer class. The prospect of a 600-acre farm, guaranteed salary of £60 a year, plus passage and all expenses paid by the employers, might well have seemed the answer to Langford's rumoured "reversal of fortunes." He would expect the life of a country squire to continue in the colonial setting of Vancouver Island as it did for so many Englishmen in India under the East India Company.

Captain Langford was the first of three British bailiffs hired by the Puget Sound Agricultural Company for their four farms. Company directors, all directors of the parent Hudson's Bay Company as well, advertised throughout England and Scotland for married men who either owned property of their own or were able to find security amounting to £30. Those selected would have charge of a farm of 600 to 700 acres, with five British labourers for every 100 acres.

Four days after the publication of this promotion in 1850 Captain Langford was at Company headquarters in London negotiating a contract which included a higher salary than advertised, and extended to 15 years. He was also entitled to a third of each year's profits from the farm, but if there were no profits, losses would be deducted from future profits of the four farms. If it sounded too good to be true – it was. (See Appendix I)

In its efforts to lure immigrants to its Pacific Coast fur trading post, the Hudson's Bay Company was known to exaggerate the attractions and amenities of the place. Employment with one of the largest global corporations known to man might well have sounded more attractive than in fact it was. The promise of large tracts of land and a guaranteed market would be attractive to gentlemen who expected to own the land eventually.

> *He was also entitled to a third of each year's profits from the farm, but if there were no profits, losses would be deducted from future profits of the four farms. If it sounded too good to be true – it was.*

Fort Victoria, begun in 1843, is shown in this illustration from Edgar Fawcett's Reminiscences of Old Victoria, published in Toronto in 1912, "showing inside of Fort from Wharf Street, 1859." (Author Collection)

Agricultural workers and their families were easily persuaded, believing that having their passage paid to a colony with guaranteed employment and, after 1852, the promise of land when they completed their contracts, would ensure a better future than tenant farming or factory work in Britain.

In fact Fort Victoria did provide some comforts of home not available to settlers in other parts of British North America. Necessary foodstuffs (and liquor) could be bought at the Sale Shop, the Company store which stocked supplies brought from England by sailing ships on their annual voyages to collect furs. Cattle, sheep and pigs were raised locally to provide meat for visiting Royal Navy ships as well as the small European population, and there were fruit orchards and vegetable gardens even in the early days of the settlement. The Company also saw to protection from unpredictable natives and provided some labour to help with land clearing

Edgar Fawcett described his first impressions of the Fort on his arrival as a young boy in 1859: "The first thing that attracted our attention… was the high palisade of the fort which ran along Wharf Street from the corner of Bastion [View Street] to Broughton, up thence to Government Street, along Government Street … Opposite Fort Street there was an entrance and another on Wharf Street. In the centre of the large gates there were smaller ones. These small gates were opened every morning at seven o'clock on the ringing of the Fort bell, which was suspended from a kind of belfry in the centre of the yard. To the north were the stores and warehouses, and to the south large barns; the residences were situated on the east side of the fort. The stores were patronized by all the colonists, not then being confined to the Company's servants, as in former times." A large

A large orchard surrounded by a whitewashed fence ran along Government Street, and the Company's bakery, a white-washed log building, was across the rough and muddy Fort Street.

orchard surrounded by a whitewashed fence ran along Government Street, and the Company's bakery, a white-washed log building, was across the rough and muddy Fort Street.

The Langford family boarded the 105-foot charter sailing ship Tory at Gravesend for the six-month voyage around Cape Horn in the winter of 1850-51. Their fellow passengers included Richard Golledge, an apprentice clerk to Chief Factor and Governor James Douglas; Charles Bayley, bailiff for the HBC Cadboro Bay farm, and his son; a number of farm workers with their families, and an "agricultural assistant," William Henry Newton, a relative of the Langford family. Captain James Cooper and his wife who travelled as supercargo (free passage for a former Company employee) were to be the Langford's neighbours when they lived at Cooper's Bilston Farm in Metchosin.

Their arrival at the eight-year-old fur trade fort on May 12 was depressing: no village, no streets, and no houses ready as promised. The Langfords were taken to a shack on Kanaka Row, now Humbolt Street, near the shores of muddy, foul-smelling James Bay, now site of the Empress Hotel. Edward Langford, his wife Flora and the girls, along with their servants, were expected to live there until a farmhouse was built. The fur trade officers apparently saw no problem with this temporary accommodation, a recurring theme in many accounts of newly arrived settlers from 1849 on. Two years later the bailiffs for Craigflower and Constance Cove farms found similar lack of preparation.

There are two very different versions of the continuing housing crisis.

Richard Blanshard, officially the first Governor of the Colony but in fact cruelly snubbed by the real power in the Colony, Chief Factor James Douglas, was outraged. His version of the situation was sent to London as he waited for the Colonial Office to end his nightmare posting.

> "The ship 'Tory' has just landed about 120 persons, all with two exceptions servants of the Hudson's Bay Company ... no preparations have been made here for their reception beyond erecting a couple of log houses or rather sheds, in these the remainder are huddled together like cattle as I have seen myself, to the number of thirty or thirty five in each shed, men and women, married and single without any kind of screen or partition to separate them. As may be supposed, great discontent exists already and will most certainly increase ..."

The Langfords were taken to a shack on Kanaka Row, now Humbolt Street, near the shores of muddy, foul-smelling James Bay, now site of the Empress Hotel.

"...no preparations have been made here for their reception beyond erecting a couple of log houses or rather sheds, in these the remainder are huddled together like cattle..."

According to Chief Factor Douglas, however, the *Tory* passengers were to have "our best attention." He wrote to London on February 24, 1851: "We are making every preparation in our power for their reception … and expect to have [dwelling houses] in a habitable state before the Tory arrives."

Douglas, who was appointed governor in 1851, appeared cheerfully unaware of problems in a May 15 letter to HBC secretary Archibald Barclay written shortly after the passengers landed:

> "I have now the pleasure of communicating for the information of the [HBC] Governor and Committee the arrival of the ship *Tory* at this Port, on the evening of the 9th inst. With the passengers and crew in perfect health, and you will be further pleased to learn that no deaths, and but one case of serious indisposition occurred during the voyage out, which was also unusually free of stormy weather, though protracted beyond the average length.

> "The *Tory* lay two days at the outer anchorage and was brought into Port on the 12th Inst. … The passengers have been landed and distributed to the various stations in this neighbourhood. Thirty men are transferred to Mr. Langford, for the Pugets Sound Companys [sic] farm near Esquimalt…

> "The New Comers appear to be all highly pleased with the Country and disposed to be useful: but as usual they are in a state of bustle and transition and no one has fairly settled to work."

"The New Comers appear to be all highly pleased with the Country and disposed to be useful: but as usual they are in a state of bustle and transition and no one has fairly settled to work."

The newcomers were not at all pleased. They were neither the first nor the last to discover that the exalted Company had, not to put too fine a point on it, lied.

Governor Blanshard, said to be a distant relative of Langford, took the family into his own slightly more civilized residence, where Flora gave birth to a son on July 24.[1] They stayed in the so-called Government House while their farmhouse was being built eight miles from the Fort, in the forest south of the HBC sawmill at Millstream Falls.

Captain Langford undoubtedly heard an unfavourable assessment of the Hudson's Bay Company's style of government from the retiring governor. Richard Blanshard had been treated shabbily by the arrogant HBC officers who ran the colony as they had their fur trading establishments. Not surprisingly, Captain Langford soon

---

1   George Langford was probably the first white male child born in the colony. Two girls, daughters of James and Mary Yates, were born before the Langfords arrived (Christ Church Cathedral baptism records)

joined the anti-company faction known as "the malcontents," which annoyed the soon-to-be Governor Douglas.

Nevertheless two years later Captain Langford took the oath of allegiance "as Magistrate and Justice of the Peace for the district of Esquimalt and 20 miles around it." Kenneth McKenzie of Craigflower, Thomas Skinner of Constance Cove Farm in Esquimalt and Thomas Blinkhorn of Metchosin (Captain Cooper's farm manager) were also appointed magistrates for their districts, according to Minutes from the Journals of the Council of Vancouver Island. No-one qualified for Sooke. In fact, Douglas soon discovered that none of his appointees was qualified – they badly bungled their first case brought by a troublesome American against upstanding John Muir of Sooke. The decision was quickly reversed.

Flora, Captain Langford's elegant wife, after her return to England in 1861. (BC Archives G-09706)

Meanwhile, the Langfords and other HBC families enjoyed a surprisingly active social life around the Fort, much of it provided by the naval officers and reciprocal entertainments at the Fort. One of the first notable social events after Langford's arrival was a lavish picnic James Douglas gave at Beacon Hill for the officers of HMS Portland, the flagship of Admiral Moresby. A few days later towards the end of August, 1851, the Admiral held an 'at home' aboard the ship in Esquimalt Harbour. Guests were ferried to the ship by the Portland's boats. The ship's band played for dancing, and refreshments were of the finest.

A theatrical evening on the frigate Trincomalee was a memorable event in 1853. Families came from the farms at Sooke and Metchosin, as well as Colwood, Craigflower and Esquimalt, for the serious and comic theatricals, then stayed at the Fort overnight. The Crimean War brought more naval ships to the Esquimalt station, on alert because of the fear of attack from Russian Alaska. The crinolined young ladies were all allowed to attend a ball on HMS President in 1854, shortly after the embarrassing defeat of Her Majesty's ships at the Russian base on the Kamchatka Peninsula.[2] Many of Victoria's young ladies like the Langford, McKenzie and Skinner daughters, would have been considered too young for balls, but their mothers agreed to let them attend. The 14 and 15-year-old midshipmen did not complain. A Governor's ball at the Fort in 1856, along with Captain Houston's party on the Trincomalee for all the Scots in the community, made for a jolly summer. The opening of the Assembly rooms in 1857 and a production of Sheridan's The Rivals by officers of the Fort the same year brought the colony's cultural standards to astonishing heights.

There was always music. Ships' bands played on board and on land for special occasions. Flora Langford played her piano at Colwood, and Mr. Tod played his violin. His daughter Emmaline had her piano too.

There were society weddings too. Cecilia Douglas married Dr. Helmcken in 1852, Martha Cheney married Captain Ella at Bilston Farm in 1855, the same year Emmaline Tod married Henry Newton of Colwood. Top of the list of hospitable homes to visit were the Langford family's *Colwood*, and the home of Supreme Court Justice David Cameron, *Belmont*, conveniently a short row across the entrance to Esquimalt Harbour from the Royal Navy anchorage. Mrs. Cameron, Governor Douglas's sister, was noted for her picnics and dances at Rodd Hill.

The Porter family lived in one of the cottages. Years later Mary Porter Cooper wrote: "While my father was building a real house for his bride and his children, near Millstream, we lived at Langford in a small cottage at the foot of the paddock. The Langford farm was a fine establishment, and of course there was a lot of entertaining at the Big House; for there were three [sic] Miss Langfords, and always a crowd of naval officers coming and going. Girls were scarce in the colony, and the Miss Langfords were very pretty. Mrs. Francis had another cottage and she did the laundry. Oh, the fine muslin dresses that used to be sent down to her to be washed!

"My sister and I would dress up in them and play lady, walking up and down the drive, smiling and mincing and switching round the long trains; while Mrs. Francis would watch at the bend of the road to see that nobody should catch us, all the time roaring with laughter."

The Langford's daughter, Mary, as she looked at about the time the family left Vancouver Island. She later married Captain Herbert Lewis. They returned to Victoria and lived in a small house on Birdcage Walk in the 1890s. Mary died in 1903. (BC Archives C-05712)

"Mrs. Francis had another cottage and she did the laundry. Oh, the fine muslin dresses that used to be sent down to her to be washed!"

2   For the story of the miscalculations and a commanding officer's suicide during this engagement see Barry M. Gough's *The Royal Navy and the Northwest Coast of North America, 1810-1914.*

Notice advertising for new tenants for Colwood farm (HBC Archives, University of Manitoba)

"Farm to Let For five years … From Sixth May next. Farm of Esquimalt The property of the Puget Sound Agricultural Company. Comprising about Six hundred Acres (Imperial) Two Hundred of which are under cultivation And at present in the occupation of E. E Langford, Esqre The houses and Farm buildings are excellent and in good condition.

The lands are well adapted for growing all descriptions of ordinary crops and the fields are well enclosed. The stock and sheep with implements of husbandry will be handed over to the incoming tenant at a valuation made and all further presentations to attention of Kenneth McKenzie, Agent, Puget Sound Agricultural Company Craigflower, 1856."

Mary describes the cottages that her family and other employees first lived in. "I remember we had open fires with a shelf on one side and grids to cook on. And many a fine dish was roasted or broiled or stewed in that primitive fashion. There was game in abundance, grouse in clouds, and deer.

The Porter family moved into their new house on Millstream Road. "It was April (date unknown, possibly 1856) and the ground all around was covered with lilies, like a big white sheet among all the blackened logs. My sister and I were dressed for the occasion in clean pinnies, and such a sight as we were in a short time! The house was a good size for those days, all made of planed logs built upright, and so close together not a breath of wind could get between them. It was lined with canvas and paper. A man by the name of Naylor built it. For neighbours we had the Simpsons, the Tylers of Yew Tree Farm, the Pikes and the Peatts.".

Captain Langford's public life continued amicably enough for a short while. He was one of four citizens appointed to the road improvement committee "to examine the country between Soke [Sooke] and Victoria for the purpose of selecting a line of road to connect those places." According to the Council minutes for April 7, 1853, the committee consisted of Langford, whose home was eight miles west of Fort Victoria on what is now Goldstream Avenue; James Cooper whose land was even farther away in Metchosin;

He was one of four citizens appointed to the road improvement committee "to examine the country between Soke [Sooke] and Victoria for the purpose of selecting a line of road to connect those places."

senior HBC official John Work who had conveniently bought an enormous amount of land near the Fort; and J. D. Pemberton, the highly qualified colonial surveyor, who lived in bachelor quarters at the Fort (and later owned all of Oak Bay that HBC officer John Tod and the Company hadn't already reserved). Langford and Cooper both knew well the need for better roads to their isolated farms.

The Langford house was finished by then. Governor Douglas thought it was rather grander than necessary, but Captain Langford hadn't been satisfied with the simple buildings that the Company considered adequate for a farmer. The would-be country squire deplored the start-up construction - "the frames of only two houses up, too close together, and the roofs with two large holes left in the middle for chimneys" which local workmen had begun. When Langford decided to start afresh with grander buildings Douglas removed the three Canadian carpenters he had assigned to the job, but the English labourers completed the work.

CAPTAIN LANGFORD'S INVENTORY

Captain Langford described his country estate in his 1854 inventory for the Hudson's Bay Company, now in the HBC archives at the University of Manitoba. It gives a good idea of the structures, stock and machinery "up to the 31st of May, 1854."

Workmen's dwellings were of timber, but the bailiff's six-room house combined timber, stone and brick with a floor area of 1,500 square feet, oiled and plastered throughout, with five fireplaces. Not long after the original house was finished Langford added a schoolroom where his sister, Miss Louisa Ellen Langford, enrolled Victoria girls of the better sort to her Academy for Young Ladies. (Two Douglas daughters, Agnes and Alice, were pupils.)

There was a back kitchen nearby, a garden protected by a picket fence, and a small bake house with a brick oven. The HBC inventory describes this complex as the centre of the farm, standing on high ground overlooking the farm buildings and cottages. Langford estimated it would be worth £1000. The workmen's cottages were said to be "far superior" to anything these families had ever lived in before. Four were one-room dwellings up to 375 square feet. Two double-room log cottages each had a fireplace and were finished

Governor Douglas thought it was rather grander than necessary, but Captain Langford hadn't been satisfied with the simple buildings that the Company considered adequate for a farmer.

...Miss Louisa Ellen Langford enrolled Victoria girls of the better sort to her Academy for Young Ladies.

Contemporary water colour painting of the Langford house, circa 1857, by Edward Parker Bedwell, master of the survey vessel HMS Plumper. Bedwell was one of many officers who were frequent guests at the house, conveniently accessible by launch across Esquimalt Harbour from the naval station. (BC Archives PDP85)

inside with plastered walls, luxurious for a log cabin. Two duplex cottages were even larger.

The main house was worthy of the furniture the family brought from England, including Flora's piano, jolted by wagon over the bumpy forest trails. The Langfords survived quite comfortably by pioneer standards even though the farming operations came far short of the Puget Sound Agricultural Company's expectations. Provisions could be purchased from the Sale Shop at the Fort, where the hospitable Captain ran up a tremendous bill, something like eight times his annual salary, according to HBC reckoning. Officers from the Royal Navy ships anchored across Esquimalt Harbour were entertained in style, and social life was not too bad, considering the entire British population around the Fort settlement was then fewer than 400.

Some excerpts show the detail and valuations of Langford's eight-page inventory:

> Dwelling house built of timber, stone and brick, containing six [rooms?] oiled and plastered throughout, with 5 brick chimneys 50 by 30. House attached containing kitchen, schoolroom, pantry and storeroom, ... plastered throughout, building of timber, stone and brick. With double chimneys 40 by 20 ... back kitchen attached, built of brick and timber. Court yard ... containing smaller bake house with brick ovens, garden enclosed with basket fences. (Valued at £1000)

Dairy and cheese house built of stone walls 18 inches thick, oiled and plastered with 3 glazed windows, fitted up inside with brick benches 24 ft by 16 ft. (£80)

Storehouses and larder built of squared timber, 12 ft by 12 ft. (£40)

Cottage built of timber 12ft by 12 ft (£12). More cottages, including a double structure worth from £20 to £140

Anxious not to leave anything out, Langford mentions everything from a wagon worth £40 to a turnip drill [a tool for making a furrow to sow seeds] worth £2, harnesses, light plough, carpenters tools, garden tools, and a shepherd's hut with chimney.

Livestock included: Sheep, £273, working oxen, £80, bulls, cows, heifers on calf, 3-year old steer, yearlings, pigs, mares, geldings foals and sucking calves, for a total of £749. Crops included wheat, peas, oats, tares valued at £338.15

Assistant Surveyor Benjamin Pearce submitted another inventory as of Feb. 16, 1855, of the fields surveyed: Lake field, Park field, Garden, Paddock, Laundry, corner field, Landing Place (at Paterson Point, Esquimalt harbour), and other cleared and planted areas of the farm.

Edward Langford's attempts to construct his English village in the forest were considered foolishly extravagant. His magnificent cowsheds, for example, stood empty when 86 cattle, shipped from Nisqually for the farm, bolted on landing, ran off into the woods and were never seen again. Sheep were a problem too, through no fault of Langford. He wrote to James Douglas blaming him for having the unfortunate animals delivered to the farm before land was cleared or fences built. The fact that they had been on the ship from Nisqually (near Tacoma) without food for several days didn't improve their condition.

When the London directors heard of Langford's reported mismanagement and his unstoppable extravagance (including the enormous unpaid bill for wine and spirits) they ordered his eviction.

Surprisingly, Douglas supported Langford. He wrote to Company officials in May, 1855:

Henry Newton, the 'agricultural assistant' who came to Fort Victoria with the Langfords, and may have been a cousin of Captain Langford, married Emmaline Tod, above. Their wedding at the Fort was a social highlight of 1855. (BC Archives photos G-00264 and A-01729)

Excerpt from James Douglas letter in support of Captain Langford, 1855. (HBC Archives, University of Manitoba)

"I take the liberty of writing to you on behalf of Mr. Langford on whom a notice ... has been lately served by the Puget Sound Company at the expiration of the current year ...

"I have on many [occasions had] differences of opinion with Mr. Langford in regard to his system of management, but I never saw any cause to complain of his attention to business. His greatest and only failing appears to be a want of energy and decision in the management of his servants who it may be truly said have, in most cases, scarcely done enough to pay for their food, which has really been the great source of expense at the farm under his charge. In his place I would have at once discharged two thirds of the number and [replaced them] with Indians who would have effected as much, at one half the cost of his English labourers.

"His establishment of servants is now reduced within reasonable bounds and I have great confidence that his farm, which really is a credit to the Colony, will now make a considerable return for the outlay.

"The improvements are all of a neat and substantial character, fully worth the estimates of them in the accompanying letter which at Mr. Langford's request I transmit for your information. The company should not regret the expense of putting up substantial buildings on their Farmsteads as they are at all times worth the cost, and will be found cheaper in the end than the temporary huts that are often put up in America, being an eyesore from the first and little better than a waste of money at any time."

Douglas adds that he does not think "the Company will find **any** of their farms on Vancouver Island profitable at the outset, and I really believe that Mr. Langford will do the Farm in his charge as much justice as any person likely to succeed him." He asks them to "kindly take his case into favourable consideration, and allow him, under certain restrictions as to expenditure, to have a further trial."

Begging them (HBC Governor Sir Andrew Colville and the directors) to check Langford's inventory, he remains, "Your faithful servant, James Douglas."

This seems a fair and favourable recommendation from the Governor who would later refer to Mr. Langford as "a person wholly unworthy of credence." Nevertheless, the Bailiff of Craigflower Farm, in his role as agent for the PSAC on Vancouver Island, prepared a notice a few months later announcing "Farm to Let". The notice from the Scottish farmer Kenneth McKenzie, dated January 10, 1856, at Craigflower is shown on page.

McKenzie seems eager to find another tenant for his fellow bailiff's farm. He tried to take possession of the farm in May, according to Langford's angry letter to him dated May 6, 1856:

> Sir:
> "In consequence of your coming up this day and stating that you took possession of Esquimalt [Colwood] Farm and the stock thereon, in the name of the Puget Sound Company, I hereby give you notice that by the terms of my agreement with the Puget Sound Company I denounce your proceedings as entirely illegal and that I do not admit of your being in possession either of the farm or the stock belonging to it."

Langford held on to the farm and his position until 1860, despite quarrels and impetuous behaviour that finally landed him in court. The farm's problems were soon surpassed by his disastrous political life. His election to the first legislative assembly of Vancouver Island in 1856 was quickly followed by Douglas's successful move to disqualify him, on the grounds that the manager of a 600 acre farm did not own the required 20 acres of land.

When Langford tried to buy land to qualify for the next election in 1860 there was a questionable mix-up connected with the surveyor-general's office. Joseph Pemberton claimed that the land in question had already been sold to A.G. Dallas, head of the HBC western division and husband of Douglas's daughter Jane. Worse, a scurrilous pamphlet was circulated purporting to be the campaign platform of a "Mr. Longford," written by person or persons unknown. Evidence points to Judge Matthew Baillie Begbie and Douglas's clerk Charles Good who later eloped with Alice Douglas.

Captain Langford was made to look a freeloading fool, his political career ruined. He brought an unsuccessful suit against the printer of the widely circulated letter, but the supposed authors of the libel were never accused. Instead, Langford was sent to jail after the disorderly hearing. To prevent humiliation of his wife and family, the authorities were persuaded to release Langford within a few hours. Friends came to his assistance – Captain G. H. Richards of HMS

The Governor would later refer to Mr. Langford as "a person wholly unworthy of credence."

Worse, a scurrilous pamphlet was circulated purporting to be the campaign platform of a "Mr. Longford," written by person or persons unknown.

Plumper and Edward Langford's friend and fellow "malcontent" James Yates were among those who raised $500 to cover his debts.

Describing the bizarre trial on his return to England, Langford complained: "The examination for the defence was carried on in my absence, evidence which I had given under oath was struck out... and a non-suit recorded. I was sentenced to be imprisoned in the common jail, and to pay a fine of £10 pounds. I was taken to prison and locked up with felons, Indians, and maniacs."

The Langfords left the Colony on January 12, 1861, their passage paid by friends, their spirits lifted by a flattering and sympathetic farewell written by Amor de Cosmos in his British Colonist – "a spirited Englishman, supporter of time-honoured usages as contrasted with the policy of a feudal corporation."[3] The 54-year-old Captain rose to fight his foes again, adding his grievances to many others before a British parliamentary committee examining the Hudson's Bay Company's management of Britain's little Pacific colony. Proceedings of this committee were dutifully reported in the British Colonist by its vociferously anti-company owner, the opinionated Amor de Cosmos.

The unflattering view of Langford as a foolish, extravagant quarrelsome man with a frivolous wife is contradicted by some of his letters available through the Hudson's Bay Company archives. His analysis of the government of the colony with suggested solutions is a well-thought out document which the exasperated Governor Douglas apparently chose to ignore. The question remains: Why did Edward Langford transplant his wife and family to a wilderness colony? Was it the first example of his faulty judgement, or an understandable wish to be part of an exciting new venture – as it was promoted, not too accurately, by the Hudson's Bay Company directors?

During all the sorry business at the end of their Colwood days, Edward Langford was called a hopeless manager, totally lacking in credibility.

There are other views from some of his allies.

Interviews with people who knew the Langfords were recorded by Nora deB. Lugrin for her 1928 book, *The Pioneer Women of Vancouver Island.* Emmaline Tod Mohun, daughter of HBC officer John Tod

---

3   The British Colonist, strongly favouring Langford over Douglas and his "family-company-compact," reported fully on the trial and the group of merchants who petitioned on Langford's behalf. They raised a substantial sum to pay for his passage back to England, which the Company had refused to do.

(her first husband was a relative of Langford), remembered the Langfords in the early 1920s when she was 93 years old:

> "They were charming people, and while I lived in Victoria I spent many a happy day with them. They had a picturesque cottage on what is now known as Langford Plaines [sic] or Colwood, a stretch of park-like country that reminded one of English scenery. I am afraid all that locality has lost its former beauty. Even the pretty cottage has been allowed to fall down from age and neglect." (The 'pretty cottage' was suffering terminal dilapidation in 1898 and was demolished around 1900. The second house built for the Wale family, who leased the farm, has also disappeared.)

> "The eldest daughter married Captain Jocelyn, R.N., who was killed in action only a few years after. She was left with a little boy who eventually joined the army and went to India."

James Deans, a Scot who was a shepherd on HBC farms at the time, included a few words on behalf of Mr. Langford in his popular Rustic Rhymes, reproduced in part with his original spelling:

> Darkest and saddest of days for our Colony
> Strongly the storms of adversity Claw
> Darkest of sable Clouds pregnant with villainy
> Hangs ower our parlement, Langford's awa ….

> Devotees of beaver skins, down with monopoly
> Musk rats and salt salmon, down with them aa
> [You] sic hearted God fearing on with your panoply
> Bring back the laddie the knaves sent awa …

> Sae as we adore him, until they restore him
> We'll hate the black Clique who has sent him awa.

Another contemporary assessment of the controversial Captain Langford comes from a young Royal Navy officer, Edmund Hope Verney. He wrote from Esquimalt in 1863 after reading about the proceedings of the House of Commons committee on Vancouver Island affairs:

> "From what I can hear of Mr. Langford, I think he must be a good sort of man. I hear that the Hudson's Bay Company treated him very badly, glutted the market when he had corn to sell, so that he could make no profit, and succeeded in nearly ruining him: but then I also hear that he was not judicious, that he made virulent attacks upon the company, and declared open war, so of course the end of it was that the weaker went to the wall: he was hospitable, popular with the navy, and of refined tastes and habits: whatever right he may

"…I am afraid all that locality has lost its former beauty. Even the pretty cottage has been allowed to fall down from age and neglect."

"…I hear that the Hudson's Bay Company treated him very badly, glutted the market when he had corn to sell, so that he could make no profit, and succeeded in nearly ruining him…"

have had on his side seems to have been thrown away by his want of tact and judgment. But of course, this is all hearsay, as I never saw him." [4]

Midshipman Verney's writings seem as fair an assessment as any of the first family of Langford. Little else is known of Edward and Flora after they left Victoria. An entry in vital statistics records at Croydon, Surrey, lists the death of Edward Edwards Langford in 1895. He was 85 years old.

The only known description of the interior of the original 1850s house is Hazel Scafe Olson's account of the days when her grandparents, William and Alice Wale, leased the farm in the 1890s. Hazel is relying on information from her aunt Daisy Wale to supplement her childhood memories. The original house was demolished sometime around 1901. Its replacement, built for the Wale family in 1898 by the HBC, suffered the same fate. (See Appendix II)

---

4   From *The Vancouver Island Letters of Edmund Hope Verney*. Verney was posted to Esquimalt for three years in command of a Royal Navy gunboat. He corresponded regularly with his father, a prominent British Member of Parliament, reporting to him on the state of the colonies of Vancouver Island and British Columbia. Verney senior sent London newspapers with reports on the parliamentary hearings about Vancouver Island. [3]

2

GOLDSTREAM GOLDRUSH

The peaceful Goldstream district has had its moments of excitement since the 1850s. The first was the 1858 'gold rush' which brought a flurry of activity to the land beyond Colwood Farm. Later it was a popular recreation destination for day-trippers and hunting parties when the Esquimalt and Nanaimo Railway was completed in 1886. The first hydroelectric generating plant in British Columbia was built there in 1898, using water from what became the principal source of domestic water for Greater Victoria.

Colonial surveyor J. D. Pemberton first walked along the unnamed stream beyond Captain Langford's farm in 1852. He described it as a major fishing ground for local Indians and mentioned some traces of gold. Interest in his report was limited, which is understandable at a time when there were fewer than 100 Europeans at Fort Victoria, nearly all of them employees of the Hudson's Bay Company.

Six years later, at the beginning of the famous Fraser River gold rush in 1858, Peter Leech of the Royal Engineers found traces of gold in the banks of the stream he called the Gold Creek. That report certainly caught the interest of miners in Victoria on their way to the big gold rush on the mainland.

Rumours that gold might be found within walking distance of the Fort appeared in Victoria's first newspapers, the Gazette and the

Photograph from Picturesque Victoria, *a promotional booklet published by T.N. Hibben, circa 1900, shows the high wooden bridge across the Goldstream River, believed to have been in approximately the same location as the present bridge.* (Author Collection)

Express, which began publishing when thousands of men arrived at the quiet little settlement en route to the Fraser River. Miners and local entrepreneurs jumped at the chance to avoid the perilous and costly journey to the Fraser River diggings. The first prospectors found their way through bush and forest trails to pan for gold in the gravel of the stream in October, 1858. Unfortunately "an overflow of water in the creek … stopped the miners before they had time to get to bedrock," a story in the Express reported.

Victoria's first newspaper editors were skeptical. Precise information about the location of the treasure was scarce so the excitement died down for the winter. Prospectors were back in August, 1859, encouraged by reports of more gold discoveries. "The most silly and idle rumors were circulated all the day, and in several bar-rooms suspicious collections of specimens of coarse gold were exhibited as having come from the new diggings on Dead Man's Creek" scoffed the Victoria Gazette.

One of the few dependable witnesses who gave the story some credibility was M. T. W. Davidson, self-styled experienced miner from California, who had been out to the creek "about 15 miles to the northwest of Victoria. He said he started out on Tuesday [two days previous] in company with some six or seven others, to discover a route to the Saanich river, upon which he heard gold had been found." (Victoria Gazette, August 26, 1859.)

On August 27 the Gazette continued the story: "We started from Victoria … taking the Craig Flower road, and keeping it until we reached Mr. Langford's farm …. Crossed his large grain field and took a trail which leads to Langford Lake."

The route they describe winds around the brow of the mountain called Mount Skirt for a mile or more, down the mountain on the north side of the creek which they thought ran from Langford Lake to Finlayson Inlet. They "found gold everywhere in good prospects" and staked their claims.

On their way back to town they met "maybe 500 people on the way to the new diggings." Or so they said. That seems to have been the end of Langford's first gold rush.

Four years later the river now known as Goldstream was in the news again. In April, 1863, the British Colonist reported that three

"The most silly and idle rumors were circulated all the day, and in several bar-rooms suspicious collections of specimens of coarse gold were exhibited as having come from the new diggings on Dead Man's Creek"

cattlemen on their way to the Cowichan Valley[1] saw two men camped on the Golden River, apparently prospecting. With renewed interest in the possibilities of another gold strike in Victoria's own back yard, Governor Douglas ordered further exploration for minerals. Four miners returned with good news. The newspapers were still cautious, but the Evening Express was enthusiastic enough to suggest the new finds should be known as the Douglas Diggings. Heavy rains delayed digging, but "the vendors of Liquor and other creature comforts were on the site within a few days."

The first claim was staked later in October. After favorable returns were reported (one miner was said to have found gold worth 25 cents in only half an hour) companies were quickly formed to stake claims along the river and higher in the mountainside where Peter Leech had inspected a promising quartz vein. The earliest companies were content with finding placer gold, others planned ambitious shafts and tunnels in the quartz veins above the river bed.

Soon there were more than 30 companies in the business. The Regina Company gave up on placer mining and staked a claim on a spur of the Douglas quartz lead. According to newspaper reports they received an assay of $196 to the ton, which encouraged investment and helped to establish the 20-member company the same day. The Discovery Company completed a ditch and began to construct a dam, expecting to begin sluicing in a few days.

Work did not go smoothly. The Ayershire Company set up a pump and windlass and bucket system to remove the water that flooded their 20-foot shaft. Others had similar problems – the Scotch Company's 25-foot shaft collapsed after hitting bedrock. Undaunted, the Canada Company optimistically began building log houses for the men and planned to improve the road.

At the end of December, after a month of dripping rainforest weather, the most promising sample assays were taken from the claim of the Washoe Company (formed by Robert Miller who was known as 'the Robinson Crusoe of the Washoe') and Thomas Parmiter's Company. The samples were so promising the Express wrote that they were said to 'eclipse anything yet found' on Vancouver Island. Amor de Cosmos, the Colonist's eccentric editor, urged

"the vendors of Liquor and other creature comforts were on the site within a few days."

---

1   The wagon trail to Cowichan continued from the Langford Plains up through the mountains on the west side of the Saanich Arm – a three day journey.

every one to continue working their claims. Favourable assays continued and a San Francisco firm predicted that it would take a least six years to work the quartz lead.

One of Victoria's early papers, the Evening Express, sent a reporter to the Goldstream Diggings. The following excerpts are from his story published on October 19, 1863.

"The distance to the small river upon which the precious metal has been found by the party of prospectors sent out by the Governor is only about two miles beyond Langford's Lake, the favourite resort of pleasure parties during the summer months. After passing the lake by the Cowichan trail which winds along its margin, the route is through first a luxuriant wood, and afterwards through a dead forest, which has evidently been desolated only a short time ago by one of those brush fires which periodically take place.

"The route begins to ascend a hill for about a mile and a half from the lake, when a view of the turbulent mountain torrent known as Gold Stream breaks upon the eye and ear as it hurries on its rapid course through a thickly wooded valley, some hundred and fifty feet below, to its outlet in the waters of the Saanich Arm.

The trail, at a moderate grade, winds down the hill, just at the foot of which the stream is crossed by a capital waggon bridge. From this point the eye of the traveller is struck immediately by signs of the hardy miner's investigations in the shape of several holes from which prospects have been taken and a rough shanty under some magnificent trees, that has sheltered either labourers of the road party hunters, or some discreet miners who have preferred to keep what knowledge they have possessed to themselves.

"Here, prospectors must leave their horses, as the rest of the journey, from the nature of the country, has to be performed on foot. About a quarter of a mile along the right bank of the stream (above the bridge) our attention was attracted by some quartz rock which we could follow for a few feet, and which presented the appearance of being a continuous vein, and a few hundred yards further on the white tent of the Governor's exploring party on the opposite bank came in view. A fallen tree making a good natural bridge, no difficulty was experienced in crossing, and then one of the stakes of the company, about thirty feet lower, attracted our attention, and we found attached the notice of the four prospectors, claiming eight hundred feet, viz. four hundred as individual claims and four hundred additional by right of discovery. [In] a hole about four feet from the stream a few handfuls of gravel ... resulted in obtaining three colours ... The largest in the first prospect the size of an ordinary pin's head. These results were considered very encouraging, and were considered to promise diggings of at least six dollars a day.

"Gold Stream presents all the appearance of a thorough mining locality, and possesses every facility for working. The claim taken up by the Governor's party might be very easily sluiced, when it will no doubt be found to yield satisfactorily."

The anonymous reporter might have been the editor himself, who had already published his belief in a rosy future with enough gold to justify a stampede and improve the failing economy of the city.

"We are satisfied that the new diggings will soon attract crowds of miners … We cannot conclude without expressing how deeply the colonists are indebted to his Excellency Governor Douglas for the fitting out and supplying the successful prospectors in the expedition which is likely to lead to such great results … shall we call it the Douglas Diggings?"

Eager entrepreneurs Joseph Spratt and John Kriemer were so impressed they built a steam powered quartz crushing machine at the corner of Government and Broughton Streets in January, 1864, to assay the ore from Goldstream. Another company proposed a quartz-crushing mill on site at Goldstream.

By June the Kennedy Company was sinking a shaft but it too filled with water. The Britannia was finding 'gold-looking stuff' in their 20-foot shaft. The Douglas Company with an open cut 50 feet long and a tunnel 27 feet deep (which may be the tunnel that still survives in the mountainside) was still trying. The Parmiter Company continued blasting and the American Company persevered. But most of the placer miners left Goldstream.

Some quartz miners remained hopeful that a cut 50 feet into the hill would show results. There was a small surge in April when an assay reported that the Regina claim would yield gold at the astonishing rate of $10,000 a ton. Governor Arthur Edward Kennedy, Douglas's successor, rode out in April, 1864, to bolster support for the mining companies, promising to consider improving the road to Goldstream. He commented on the condition of the road, looked at most of the claims and was apparently impressed with the progress of the diggings.

Alas, the Goldstream diggings were already in decline. Investors decided it might be advisable to investigate the claims and prepare an independent report for the Governor and the House of Assembly.

Store at Kennedy Flats, Leechtown, supplied wines, liquors and cigars in 1866. It must have been an arduous journey by horseback or wagon for the lady in the crinoline with the too-high hoop. Peter Leech, a member of an expedition sent to investigate the Goldstream claims, found a gold-bearing quartz-vein about 10 miles inland in the Sooke Hills along the river that bears his name. The mining town flourished for a few years in the 1860s and attracted hopeful prospectors well into the 1930s. Hopes were dashed after Government mining engineers published a discouraging report for the Geological Survey of Canada. (BC Archives A-04474)

This report was not encouraging. The Goldstream diggings were abandoned for the more promising quartz vein farther inland at Leech River.

The Goldstream Quartz Crushing Company was wound up in April, 1865. A few sporadic efforts were made to work some of the old claims, but mining was pretty well at an end in Langford until the late 1890s, when ambitious copper mining operations began on Mount Skirt.

Some good came from these years of activity: the government road over the mountains was improved, much to the relief of the farming and missionary families at Cowichan whose only land route to Victoria was this tortuous wagon road until the railway went through in 1886, and the Malahat Highway was built along the west side of Saanich Inlet in 1911.

3

THE GOLDSTREAM HOTEL

The Goldstream district "is situated in a northeasterly direction from Esquimalt, has an area of nearly thirty square miles. It derives its name from a beautiful stream of water which flows through it, and on which gold ledges have been discovered in several places. In the southern part of the district are some good farms, and Goldstream House, distant about 12 miles from Victoria, a favorite country resort of the people of that city. It is situated on the banks of the Goldstream which affords good trout fishing. Plenty of game is found by hunters in the neighboring hills, and the summits of these latter command fine views of the Saanich Arm."
(Victoria City Directory, 1882)

The Goldstream House was built in 1885-86 to take advantage of the newly completed Esquimalt and Nanaimo Railway. The Goldstream Station was a short walk away for Sunday train excursionists. (City of Victoria Archives, 98109-16-7425)

Unfortunately for Victoria, Ottawa chose a ramshackle little collection of mills on the mainland, later known as Vancouver, as the end of the line, thus saving a great deal of money and antagonizing the Island populace.

In 1861 Victoria grew into a city of merchants and entrepreneurs who built grand houses to complement the grander ambitions of these upwardly mobile inhabitants. The obsolete fur trading fort came down in 1864, the old Governor retired, and Victoria was soon "the San Francisco of the North."

There was no boom in Langford. It dozed on for the next decade as if unconnected to the nearby capital city. It might have escaped notice for many more years, except for a broken Ottawa promise, a Scottish coal baron and an Irish entrepreneur.

The Canadian Government reneged on its promise to build a railway across Canada as part of the deal to persuade the Pacific Colony of British Columbia to join the Dominion. Unfortunately for Victoria, Ottawa chose a ramshackle little collection of mills on the mainland, later known as Vancouver, as the end of the line, thus saving a great deal of money and antagonizing the Island populace. The original plan to extend the tracks north to Bute Inlet, across the water and down Vancouver Island to Victoria, would have cost far too much. In the scramble to find private interests willing to build an island railway and put an end to west coast grumblings, coal baron Robert Dunsmuir surfaced as the logical choice. Rich beyond words from his Vancouver Island coal mines and other interests, he would also benefit from an island railway to transport coal – and from one of the largest land bribes ever negotiated in Canada. He also had wealthy San Francisco investors to share the expense.

1910: Crowds hurry down the hill from Goldstream Station between the rows of trees planted in 1886 by James Phair (Harry Rant photo).

Dunsmuir built the railway, which crossed the Langford Plains to Goldstream and over the mountains to the north.

The Daily Colonist of April 1, 1886, reported on the first trip on the Island Railway organized by Dunsmuir for his distinguished guests, members of the legislature "and other gentlemen to the number of over fifty" on board to "make a trip of inspection as far as the line was completed." Two cars decorated with bunting and propelled by a powerful Schenectady locomotive "started off at a lively pace amid favorable encomiums upon the evenness of the track, which prevented the jarring motion inseparable from travel on certain lines. ... After a run of little over half an hour, the end of the continuous track – a distance of some eleven or twelve miles – was reached. This was at a spot known as the double-headed ravine through which runs what is now known as Waugh's creek. Across this ravine is being built a trestle work some 400 feet long and 124 feet in height. Thirty-five men have been at work on this for five weeks, and in the same number of days the structure, which is built in three tiers and looks like a perfect network of bracing, will have been completed. A wire rope which is stretched across the chasm is used as a means for passing out the timber ..."

2001: The saplings have grown into the giants shown in this 2001 photo of Humpback Road.
(M. Duffus photo)

The photo of the first train to Goldstream shows the dignitaries on a flatbed car in front of the train at the end of the completed section of the tracks – an historic occasion with flags draping the locomotive and the car. (BC Archives A-01596)

The dignitaries left the train to walk along a footpath to the far side of the ravine to see tracks which continued to the Niagara Canyon. Another higher trestle was built soon after Mr. Dunsmuir's first excursion trip, which the Colonist writer described as "a most creditable piece of work, the excellence of the ballasting causing the travel to be most pleasant."

Mr. O. C. Hastings was on hand for one of Vancouver Island's first publicity photo opportunities, and "brought his camera to bear on the party and took an instantaneous photograph. This completed, the signal was given and the cars again started for Esquimalt, making a stop at Parson's bridge, where a visit was paid to the new water-works at Thetis lake." The party returned to Esquimalt where they were served a "substantial cold lunch" on the steamer which would take them back to Victoria and enthusiastic cheers for Mr. Dunsmuir, host of "a most pleasurable trip to all who partook in it."

But it was an Irish entrepreneur[1] who had the foresight to buy a half-interest in an old coaching inn on Humpback Road. The purchase included a thousand acres of land between the railway and Goldstream River. Far-sighted James Phair turned the primitive 1860s coach stop into a grand country resort near Goldstream Station. Soon after the railway was completed in 1886 crowds of Victorians boarded the train for excursions to the scenic beauties of the countryside.

Engine on the Waugh Creek Bridge, completed shortly after Dunsmuir's guests saw it on the first trip on the railway on April 1, 1886. (BC Archives D-03933)

---

1   The Irishman had some experience providing comfort for travellers. When he first settled on a cattle ranch in the picturesque Nicola Valley, near Merritt in the interior of British Columbia, James Phair married Mary Gilmore, daughter of a neighbouring rancher. When the road to Merritt was built Phair's ranch house became a stopping place for travelers in that area. After a decade of successful ranching and inn-keeping the Phairs moved to Victoria, where Mary's father already owned the Goldstream land.

For more than two decades a train excursion to Goldstream House and its scenic surroundings was a favourite Sunday outing. Passengers at Goldstream Station wait for the return train to Victoria.

Picnickers wait for coffee brewed by hotel staff at the side of the hotel.

Ticket seller for the Goldstream excursion trains. These pictures were taken by Harry Rant in 1910 and lent for publication by Derek Orchard.

Thanks to the railway and some finely tuned public relations efforts, the day-trippers came in droves. Land was cleared, trees were felled, huge water tanks behind the hotel supplied all the water needed, and Mary Phair helped to give the place the friendly welcoming atmosphere Victorians enjoyed. James Phair and his workmen built trails through the woods down to the river. He also allowed the militia to use his fields as a firing range, ensuring more thirsty customers in the saloon after rifle practice.

Phair's first brilliant public relations move was made with the cooperation of the traffic manager of the railway,

With the round trip fare at an affordable 25 cents, the Goldstream excursion specials are said to have carried "fully a thousand people … both trains being well filled with holiday makers."

The morning train left at 9 o'clock. Thoughtfully, the railway put on a 2 p.m. train as well for those who felt they must attend morning church services. Soon Wednesday evening concerts featuring the band of the Fifth Militia Regiment and other attractions were popular

Gentlemen gather at The Goldstream House, suited and bowler-hatted potential customers for the popular British style saloon.
(BC Archives C-03752)

"This house, situated at Goldstream, is the terminus of pleasure-seekers of perhaps the most beautiful drive around Victoria."

as well. (A few long-time residents remember the remains of the octagonal bandstand on the corner of Humpback Road, site of a small grocery store and coffee shop in 2003.)

By 1891 the hotel was so well-established that it earned favourable mention in an early promotional publication, *Victoria Illustrated:* "This house, situated at Goldstream, is the terminus of pleasure-seekers of perhaps the most beautiful drive around Victoria. The genial proprietor, Mr. James Phayer [sic] who has been established here some six years has made the house exceedingly popular. In addition to the beautiful strolls around his house, the stream and woods in the vicinity abound with trout, pheasant, grouse deer, bear and about anything the huntsman may desire. Mr. Phayer is himself an ardent sportsman and is always willing to accompany his guest on a hunting expedition. He is a young man, a large property owner, and has bought one thousand acres of land, of which he has 100 acres under cultivation."

Dominion Day Picnic

Not all picnics centered around the Goldstream House activities. One gigantic picnic stood out for seven-year-old Hazel Scafe, eldest daughter of William and Alice Scafe. Dixi Ross, the well-known Victoria grocer, and other prominent merchants organized a huge gathering at Goldstream to celebrate Dominion Day in 1906. Hazel wrote about this memorable occasion many years later:

"Three thousand participants came on the trains that shuttled back and forth during the day between the city and Goldstream fields and the Flats..."

"Festivities organized by several prominent Victoria merchants were a great success. Employees of Dixi Ross, operator of an outstanding food and liquor store, sponsored and organized most of the events which featured a variety of sports and activities. Scafe family members were regular customers of the Dixi Ross store when we lived at Esquimalt. Father received a personal invitation to attend the picnic with his family for the Dominion Day celebration. Three thousand participants came on the trains that shuttled back and forth during the day between the city and Goldstream fields and the Flats, while buggies, spring wagons, lumber wagons, bicycles and horses arrived over the dusty roads throughout the sweltering heat of the day. Our family left from Esquimalt by train, a special treat, boarding at the Naval Hospital stop at Admirals Road crossing. Mrs. Dixon, nee Emma Pike, met us at Goldstream Station with her spring-wagon, to take us up to her farm property at Goldstream Cross Road. We boarded the train early with boxes of food not ordinarily common fare for the Dixon family, such as canned tomatoes, peaches, canned pork and beans, ham, biscuits, crackers and cheese, butter, canned milk, canned salmon, sardines and lime juice with sugar to drink. 'Luxuries' for the isolated Dixon family. Plus roast beef and hard-boiled eggs. My sister was sick in the wagon all over the back of a lady's dress. Embarrassing. White, filmy, summery with pink flowers. Dozens of autos and motorcycles joined the crowd, clouds of dust. Some of the men walked the short distance to the beer parlor to escape the heat and dust. The Dixon boys Ted and Bill kept their greatest treasure and pleasure, a gramophone, playing all day long. A favourite was 'Who threw the overalls in Mrs. Murphy's Chowder' which my father referred to later as 'that confounded thing.' Mrs. Dixon later planted her geraniums in the empty tomato, peach and pork and bean cans. The sports field was near the railroad station. Young and old alike enjoyed the Fat Man's and Fat Lady's races and all sorts of other activities."

By the end of summer picnicking was out and hunting very much in. Weekend parties arrived and enjoyed the hotel's saloon, designed as an English pub so pleasing to many British Victorians. The grand Goldstream House was destroyed by fire in 1923. Mr. Phair's wooded trails are now part of the campground at Goldstream Provincial Park.

"My sister was sick in the wagon all over the back of a lady's dress. Embarrassing..."

Dixi Ross, with his staff in the popular grocery store, was one of the merchants who sponsored a gala First of July picnic in 1906.
(BC Archives F-06964)

Picnickers at Goldstream Station, (a Church of England Young People's group), around 1898, looking north along the tracks lined with huge stacks of cordwood to keep the locomotive boilers stoked on the steep climb over the Malahat Mountain.
(BC Archives A-9134)

Ladies dressed in light coloured gowns and best hats for this Orangeman's picnic in 1906, in spite of sooty smoke from the engine taking their flatbed car to Goldstream. (BC Archives D-03405)

4

GOLDSTREAM GENERATING PLANT

An agreement between the directors of the British Columbia Electric Railway Company (or just B.C. Electric Company)   and the Esquimalt Water Works Company led to construction of the first hydro power generating plant on Vancouver Island.

The 22 year-old British Columbia Electric Company power generating plant at Goldstream was photographed in the 1920s. Water used by the plant was measured by instruments in the beehive-shaped structure to the right of the water flowing into a culvert returning to the watershed system. (BC Archives I-52551)

The Goldstream plant was begun in 1897 to augment an unreliable steam powered generating system used from 1890 to supply power for the city's street lights. Robert McMicking's 25-horsepower system running on steam from coal or wood furnaces couldn't produce enough power for the Victoria Electric Railway Company's streetcars.

Wealthy Victoria businessman Frank Barnard, later Sir Frank and Lieutenant-Governor of British Columbia from 1914 to 1919, was a major mover in the Consolidated Railway and Light Company which bought up three bankrupt streetcar companies in Victoria, Vancouver and New Westminster. Englishman Robert Horne Payne was responsible for finding British investors for Consolidated, which later became the B.C. Electric Railway Company.

The company negotiated use of water from Cabin Pond, a small reservoir in the Waugh Creek watershed at Goldstream, 14 miles from town. Construction began on the building near Japan Gulch 1897 and was completed in 1898.

The building in 2002, still standing undisturbed in the forest in the restricted Goldstream watershed, abandoned but still an impressive structure at 113 years old.
(M. Duffus)

Construction of the power house was a tremendous undertaking in the last years of the 19th century. There were no power-operated machines like bulldozers and graders, nor any decent roads to Goldstream. As T. R. Meyers points out in his 1955 history, *The Public Utility Service on Vancouver Island,* "Human brawn and muscle and straining horse flesh had to make up for such deficiencies.

Frank Barnard, a major player in the early days of the BC Electric Railway Company, was the son of Francis Jones Barnard, owner of the Barnard Express which controlled most of the transport between Victoria and the British Columbia gold fields during the Fraser river gold rush (BC Archives G-08024)

Early photo of Goldstream generating plant shows water diverted downhill to the generators from a small reservoir in the Waugh Creek watershed. The plant is thought to have been one of the first 'high-head' or high-pressure plants on the Pacific coast. Up to that time hydro plants operated with a head of water of from 40 to 100 feet, but the Goldstream project operated under a static head of 700 feet that delivered water at 285 pounds per square inch to the Pelton wheels that drove the generators, according to T. R. Meyers in his 1955 history of public utilities on Vancouver Island. (BC Archives C-09651)

"Heavy equipment evidently was shipped on the Esquimalt and Nanaimo Railway to Goldstream Station, from which point the power house was a relatively short distance away. From that point on, men and horses took over. Planks were laid on the road … and the heavy items of equipment were inched, with the aid of block and tackle, to their final resting place in the power house."

The Consolidated company owned nothing but the power house. Water driving the turbines was the property of the Esquimalt Water Works and was measured in a beehive structure as it made its way from the upper levels of the watershed to lower reservoirs. The original plant consisted of two 360 kilowatt, or 600 horsepower, generators. A 500 kilowatt generator was soon added, and in 1904 a 1,000 kilowatt unit was installed.

The plant is thought to have been one of the first 'high-head' or high-pressure plants on the Pacific coast.

Early operators at the Goldstream plant were R. H. Sperling, later manager of the company in Vancouver; G. M Tripp who became general superintendent of the Vancouver Island division, and E. Davis who was Comptroller of Provincial Water Rights in later years.

The company set about securing rights-of-way all over Victoria to distribute its electricity. Many of these are still in existence from Langford through Esquimalt, much to the surprise of property owners. One landowner who refused to allow the plant access to his property was James Phair of the Goldstream Hotel, who got a court injunction against the company.

Ironically, the B.C. Electric Railway Company was partially responsible for the decline in guests at Mr. Phair's Goldstream House resort. The 1905 opening of the Company's amusement park on the Gorge waterway, conveniently located at the end of a streetcar line, saw more than 3,000 Victorians arrive at the "fairyland of sylvan beauty lit by countless electric lamps and enlivened by the strains of a good military band." *(Colonist report)* This nearby playground, made even more accessible by the availability of automobiles and improved city roads, eventually drew customers away from the Goldstream House as a popular Sunday outing.

The little power plant at Goldstream couldn't keep up with demand for electric power for long. The Jordan River plant, 27 miles away, began supplying power in 1911. The B.C. Electric Company was sold to a Montreal-based company in 1928.

A newspaper reporter visited the Goldstream plant in 1955, shortly before it was to be shut down forever:

> "After sixty years of producing electricity for Victoria, the roaring generators of the 1898 hydro plant at Goldstream fell silent, to be used again only in emergencies. The Jordan River plant and the new submarine cable from the mainland could produce power more inexpensively, but until the mid 1950s the original plant, state of the art in 1898, was still put to use as a backup in peak load periods.

> "Doomed a dozen times since it began operating in 1898, the Goldstream hydro plant of the B.C. Electric Railway Company will see another period of activity in December and January [of 1955[before the mainland cable planned for next year sounds its death knell once and for all time."

During the interview Ira F. Smith, special assistant to the company's light and power superintendent, explained: "We think it's

Now all is quiet in the off-limits forest of the watershed, in the century-old building where the water rushed down the hill to the roaring generators, and out again to be measured on its way to the reservoirs.

finished, then something happens and we find it is handy to have around." Shortly before that 1955 interview the plant was in operation during a washout of a portion of the flume serving the Jordan River plant. The Goldstream unit was put to use during all peak load periods until the flume was replaced, and even in quiet periods was "limbered up and ready for emergencies" for a few more years.

Now all is quiet in the off-limits forest of the watershed, in the century-old building where the water rushed down the hill to the roaring generators, and out again to be measured on its way to the reservoirs.

When the plant's capacity was raised to the staggering 1,000 kilowatts in 1904 B.C. Electric Company officials and a group of prominent citizens made the trip to Goldstream to mark the occasion. A newspaper report of the time claimed that after a thorough inspection of the of the plant "insulators were filled to the brim with aerated waters from the famous springs of G. H. Mumm and Company, and the health and success of the new unit was heartily honoured." The group of ladies and gentlemen pictured above were guests at a different occasion in 1907. (Victoria City Archives 98102-04-1633)

Strange object in the Goldstream forest is the structure that measured the water flow billed to the BC Electric generating plant for their use from a resevoir of water owned by the Esquimalt Water Works (M. Duffus photo, 2001)

5

Copper Mines on Skirt Mountain

Little more than a decade after his successful launch of the Goldstream Hotel, James Phair was involved in a new enterprise. One of the hotel's regular customers was William Ralph, listed as a civil engineer and surveyor in an 1877 Victoria directory. He had been exploring the local area, including Skirt Mountain (also referred to as Mount Skirt) about a mile northeast of the hotel on the other side of Goldstream River, for several years.

Remains of old shacks on the Goldstream Flats, first identified as old Indian dwellings, might have been the Chinese mineworkers' cabins seen by Billy Payne in 1902. (View Royal Archives, Pearce collection photo, ca. 1906, attributed to Duncan McTavish)

Mr. Phair was quick to invest when Mr. Ralph needed money to test his claim for copper deposits on the mountain. Theodore Lubbe, a Victoria furrier who was also a gold fever veteran, joined soon after. Wine merchant Andrew Tolmie, one of the lucky miners at the Cassiar gold diggings, was the fourth member of the Ralph Mining Company who registered four claims in their own names on Skirt Mountain on December 1, 1897. A December 17 *Colonist* article about the mining activity gave James Phair credit for restraint:

> "Every foot of ground in the vicinity of Goldstream has, within the last few weeks, been taken up by enthusiastic prospectors, stakes running like a low picket fence all along the base of the mountain – while even on Mount Finlayson some distance away, numerous locations have been made. The present excitement is based almost entirely upon the results following the persistent work of Mr. James Phair and his three associates. They have steadily refrained from talking of their discoveries and still are reticent, although Mr. Phair admits that his brightest dreams of mineral wealth of his district appear on the eve of realization. 'It will be time enough to speak,' he says, 'when we have proved the worth of our property and commence to develop it on a large scale'."

The hoped-for bonanza was "advantageously situated on a railway line and within twelve miles of Victoria." The Colonist also reported that the partners were offered a large sum in cash for their claims but refused to sell.

A prodigious amount of work was carried out over the next two years. Annual reports of the Provincial Minister of Mines record that a 25-foot shaft was completed by the end of 1897. The 1899 report indicates more than 1300 feet of work completed at a cost of $13,000, and an assay of 18 to 25 per cent copper, one ounce of gold and fifty cents in silver was returned. Two hundred tons of high-grade ore had been removed from the main ledge, and 500 tons of second grade ore from another. Six men were reported working on the 160-foot shafts and 100 feet finished along the chute of ore.

A year later the Pacific Steel Company searched the mountain for ore for the steel industry, but a number of open cuts led them to conclude that the ore was too contaminated with copper to be of any use to them. Ralph and Tolmie sold their shares of the company but Phair and Lubbe continued, completing 400 feet of drift shafts and crosscuts with 11 men employed. All showed payable ore. An aerial tramway carried the ore down the mountain to the road.

A young visitor to the mines, Billy Payne, described the workings in 1902:

> "In those days when you crossed the Goldstream wagon road you came to flats … Some Chinese who were working for Jim Phair were living in cabins there … where the mine was bringing down ore by cable. We climbed to the mine entrance, and there to the left of the mouth, was a blacksmith shop – a sort of lean-to with a forge for sharpening drills and picks … A narrow-gage railway operated in the passageway which stretched for 30 feet until it came to a big cavern … a sort of pocket. A deep shaft fell from the floor of the cavern."

Billy looked down from the rim at the top where Charlie Woodruff, a miner employed by Phair, took him to the edge of the shaft: "As I peered into that dark column, I could see two flicks of light from the miner's caps. We shivered. It was cold in there, and we were glad to get back to the entrance where the little cars were dumping ore." The ore was put into sacks and let down on a heavy cable which ended under two big cedar trees. "There it was loaded onto mules. Some of these mules could take four to five hundred pounds of ore. The mules packed the ore to the wagons which in due course carried the stuff to the smelter."

This burst of activity came to an end in 1903 when the Ralph Mining Company found the ore was too contaminated with magnetite (magnetic iron oxide) to be worth more investment. Twenty years later, in 1924, S. P. Moody Jr. and others secured a lease and bond on the old Ralph Group. The syndicate hoped that new technology, such as electrical pumps for keeping the shaft clear of water, would make it possible to dig a lower tunnel to drain the mine. They cleared away the old workings and sent five samples for assay, but nothing came of these efforts. The bond was allowed to lapse.

Mineral rights for two of the four Ralph Company claims are still held by a family for a small annual payment. Parts of the claims overlap the present boundaries of Goldstream Provincial Park.

There are only a few traces of the mine shafts, donkey trails and single gauge railway now, but British Columbia Hydro found another use for the historic mining and hunting area in the 1970s: a line of heavy-duty steel towers marches up over the top and down again, carrying electricity to Greater Victoria.

They found the entrance to the "wonderful cavern" a natural shaft about 10 feet in diameter hidden in the wild wood undergrowth.

Another feature of Skirt Mountain intrigued prospectors in 1899. The story of the legendary subterranean lake was reported to the Victoria *Daily Times* in 1899 by two ex-Klondike miners "prospecting in the neighbourhood of the Langford Plains." Their "mysterious pond in the heart of the mountain" made newspaper headlines as a "Strange Find At Goldstream." The Peterson brothers claimed they found a passage opening into a large chamber where inky blackness prevailed. By the light of their candles they estimated that the icy cold fresh water lake extended far into the distance.

Soon after their story was published a reporter from a rival newspaper spent a Sunday afternoon exploring Skirt Mountain with friends and found the size of the "lakelet" was greatly exaggerated. "The mysterious subterranean sheet of icy water is about one mile from Langford Lake, or a mile and a half from Goldstream House. Perhaps one third of the distance from the road there is an excellent

Skirt Mountain and the other hills and mountains around Langford were favourite hunting grounds from the 1890s. These sportsmen were photographed on the Langford Plains in 1906 during a hunting weekend in the district. Newspapers reported on special prizes donated by merchants for a similar picnic sponsored by the Victoria Gun Club: Thomas Plimley donated a bicycle lamp, J. Barnsley sporting goods, a hunting knife, C. W. Rogers a box of chocolates, Paterson Shoe Co., a pair of hunting boots, Victoria book and Stationery a wolf's head inkstand. Other prizes were a Christie hat, a razor strop, a pocket knife, a hunting knife from sports goods merchants Pichon & Lenfesty, a roast of beef from R. Porter and sons and a bottle of Scotch from the Windsor Grocery. (BC Archives B-04107)

mountain trail which passes the Phair and West mines … After Mr. West's mine has been lost to sight there comes … a plunge through dense underbrush and wild vines, a scramble down and up deep ravines, a taste of cedar swamp …" and precipitous cliffs. They found the entrance to the "wonderful cavern" a natural shaft about 10 feet in diameter hidden in the wild wood undergrowth. They reached "a cave of very respectable dimensions" but were disappointed that the cave and lake ended only 40 to 50 feet away. The water was not more than six feet deep according to their measurements.

The *Colonist* story added another oddity to the lore of Skirt Mountain. The teetering rock, weighing several tons was "so nicely poised that it can be moved up and down with the strength of one man's arm."

John Goudy lives at the north end of Florence Lake and walks along the trails of Skirt Mountain. He confirms that the opening of the tunnels can still be seen in 2003 and that the underground lake exists.

6

TWO PIONEER LANGFORD FAMILIES

In 1891, when the popular Goldstream Hotel was the only attraction worth the trip to Langford, William Wale was negotiating with the Hudson's Bay Company for a lease on Captain Langford's old farm. The 600 acres and the original house were still more or less intact and still owned by the HBC. At the same time the John H. Scafe family was living a few miles north, in the house John H. and his father-in-law built on the shores of a Highland lake in 1874. The marriage of John Scafe's son William to William Wale's daughter Alice in 1898 united the two pioneer families whose descendants still live in Langford. Their story covers more than a century of Langford history.

THE WALE FAMILY

William Wale was 10 years old when he arrived at Victoria in 1853 aboard the *Norman Morison* on the same voyage that brought the Kenneth McKenzie and Thomas Skinner families to the Puget Sound Agricultural Farms, Craigflower and Oaklands. With his mother and stepfather, Edmund Austin Williams, he stayed at the Fort where his step- grandfather, Edmund Williams, worked for the Hudson's Bay Company. Young William Wale also worked for the Company for five years, herding sheep and cattle at the Company's Uplands Farm.

At the age of 30 on October 10, 1872, he married Ann McHugh, the 22-year-old daughter of a prosperous Saanich family. The couple lived in a log house on the shores of Elk Lake near Ann's parents for the first 10 years of their marriage. They left the Elk Lake property for

Information in this chapter is based on a collection of stories and photographs compiled by Hazel Scafe Olson, a granddaughter of William and Alice Wale. Hazel died in March, 1990, in her 91st year. The unpublished two-volume history of the families was edited by her son Almer Olson.
(Scafe/Wale photo)

William Wale, tenant at Captain Langford's farm in the 1890's.
(Scafe/Wale collection)

With the proceeds of the Elk Lake sale they bought Yew Tree Farm, a landmark on Millstream Road.

Langford in 1882 when the city of Victoria, fearing pollution of its major water supply from livestock grazing near the lake, made an acceptable offer for the acreage.

With the proceeds of the Elk Lake sale they bought Yew Tree Farm, a landmark on Millstream Road. The property had been the home of Caleb Pike, another pioneer who came to Fort Victoria in the early 1850s for the Hudson's Bay Company. He advertised it for sale in 1862:

"To be sold, let or leased, Yew Tree Farm, situated two miles from Esquimalt Harbour, consisting of 268 acres of land with an abundance and constant stream of fresh water, dwelling house, barn, stables and out houses. About nine tons of hay, and present crops. Farm utensils of all kinds. One half under fence. For further particulars apply to Bailey's Grocery store, or Caleb Pike, on the premises."

According to Hazel Olson's records an Englishmen called Tyler bought it from Caleb Pike and offered it for sale again 20 years later. William and Ann Wale found it to be "most desirable" and lived there for eight years. They specialized in raising poultry, supplying geese and turkeys to the well patronized Goodacre's meat market where Ann's brother-in-law, John Dooley, was a partner. (He was married to Ann's sister Mary Elizabeth Wale – 'Aunt Dooley' to Alice and the other Wale children.)

The enterprising William Wale tried many business ventures. He hired Chinese workmen to cut cordwood which they stacked in huge piles nine to 12 feet high along a quarter-mile length of Millstream Road.[1] The wood was delivered by horse-drawn wagon for household heating and cooking. Another profitable venture was selling charcoal, which he made in a cave on the farm, as a purifying agent for the city water supply from Elk Lake. Ann did many of the farm chores, raising calves, sheep, pigs and poultry which she and William either butchered and dressed themselves or sold directly to the slaughter house in View Royal.

William and Anne sold this prosperous farm in 1890 to a Dr. Hannington and moved briefly to a 100-acre farm in the McHugh valley, bought with the $35,000 proceeds from the Yew Tree Farm sale. Two years later William and Ann were back in Langford again, this time at Captain Langford's original farm.

---

1   *This stretch of road is part of the four lane divided highway now called Veterans Memorial Parkway*

Carriages line the fence and spectators watch in the rain at a steeplechase meet on William Wale's race track in the 1890s. The former sheep pasture was an attractive setting for race meets that brought well dressed crowds from the city for several seasons in the 1890s. William cleared stones from the fields and thousands of the larger rocks were removed with a horse and stoneboat, improving the grazing for sheep as well as leveling a suitable racetrack. Golfers at the Royal Colwood course used to notice piles of stones heaped around the foot of many of the old oak trees, unaware that they were gathered from the surrounding flat land by William as he prepared the track. One little pile of rocks is just visible in the lower right corner above. (BC Archives H-02413 and F-03250)

The house and farm had been leased in 1862, shortly after Captain Langford's disgrace and departure, and again in 1866. Early advertisements, quoted in Hazel's history of the farm, claim that the farm was equipped with garden, attached servant's quarters, a flock of sheep and water frontage with a landing pier. After 30 years and a number of tenants, including the Knox family and the Thomas Atkins family, the house was not in great shape.

The Hudson's Bay Company agreed to lease the home and property to William Wale after 'Grandmother Atkins' died there in 1891. Although the Company asked the rather steep rent of $400 a year,

It took a week to transport all the family possessions, animals, tools and machinery back to Langford in loaded lumber wagons.

The only traces of original buildings left after the house was demolished were the foundations of the stone dairy, described in detail in Captain Langford's inventory.

the lease was signed and the Wale family moved in. It took a week to transport all the family possessions, animals, tools and machinery back to Langford in loaded lumber wagons.

William cleaned up the land and repaired run-down fencing. The new split-rail fences, zigzagging and crisscrossing over the usable acres, separated the gardens from the livestock so sheep and cattle could graze at will. Many older residents remembered shortcutting across the fields to school. Some mention the cows, others the race track, and encounters with cougars which were called pumas in earlier days.

Great improvements were made to the land but the old house was nearing its end. The Hudson's Bay Company agreed to build a new house nearby for its tenants, but the original home stood long enough for a young granddaughter, Hazel, to remember and record her recollections half a century later. (Appendix II)

The only traces of original buildings left after the house was demolished were the foundations of the stone dairy, described in detail in Captain Langford's inventory. They were still standing in 1971. The dairy was used by Ann Wale for storing milk, meat or dairy produce. She insisted on keeping several good milk cows to supply her need for top grade butter, her specialty, and to feed hungry calves for market.

Hazel Scafe Olson wrote about her Grandmother Wale working in the old dairy Captain Langford built.

"I can still visualize Grandmother Wale with a cream skimmer in her hand, transferring that thick, yellowish, heavy cream into a bowl. Her tool was a thin, wide, slightly beveled tin instrument with perforations on the surface, allowing the milk to run through while the cream remained in the skimmer. Several wide tin milk pails, some almost eighteen inches in diameter and eight inches deep, lined the shelves of the dairy. Grandmother Wale also made cheese at the farm. She heated milk in the huge copper boiler, tested for temperature, then added [a curdling agent called] rennet. As the curds separated from whey, they were removed from the heat, poured through the strainer, then into presses lined with cheesecloth while clamps were tightened to remove the remaining whey. Somehow she knew when to remove cheeses from the press. Pieces were wrapped and waxed and stored in the dairy for curing. Granny was reluctant to allow anyone entrance to her milk house. She was clean and meticulous when it came to preparation and handling of dairy products and meats, and made it clear that the same was expected of everyone.

Foundations of original dairy building described in Captain Langford's inventory remained well into the 20th century.
(BC Archives G-00994)

Her reputation for fine quality dairy products, particularly butter, was widespread. She was always on guard against contamination, diplomatically showing visitors out without offending. I remember feeling privileged to be allowed to peek in at the open door of the dairy on one special occasion. I still have an earthenware bowl, one of many she used to set milk in to cool. It is about fourteen inches across and four inches deep, white inside, with yellow glaze. The same type of bowl was used for baking her delicious rice or bread puddings which we often had when we visited. Grandfather Wale, noted for bargain hunting, bought a number of these bowls, some of which were "slightly misshapen near the rim."

Sometime during the years at Yew Tree Farm and the Colwood Farm the Wale family met their neighbours, the John H. Scafes.

THE SCAFE FAMILY

John H. Scafe and Elizabeth McKenzie were married in Australia on July 18, 1866. Both families had immigrated to Canada in the early 1800s, but the McKenzies left to try their luck in New South Wales, Australia. John followed to marry Elizabeth. After eight years of moving around from Australia to Kansas and Illinois, they arrived in Victoria with their older children in 1874.

(Scafe/Wale photo)

The bill of lading itemizes the furniture, including a clock and a collapsible baby's high chair that could be converted into a rocking chair to hold two small children.

Victoria was a prosperous 13-year-old city and British Columbia was a new province of the Dominion of Canada when John H. Scafe, his wife Elizabeth and their young family came to Vancouver Island in 1874.

Elizabeth's parents, the Donald McKenzies, persuaded the Scafes to sell their profitable Illinois farm and join them on Vancouver Island. John H. and Elizabeth auctioned their livestock at a two-day sale, sold the farm for the substantial sum of $2,300 in gold, and set out by train for San Francisco, then by ship to Victoria. The $30 fare on the SS Pacific seemed high, but acceptable "as part of the cost of beginning a new life."

Their granddaughter Hazel found records of the possessions brought from the Illinois farm: household items, tools, clothing, books, and a few family treasures; musical instruments (a violin, mandolin and zither), a mahogany and brass cribbage board, a set of dominoes, the family bible and an as-new White sewing machine. The bill of lading itemizes the furniture, including a clock and a collapsible baby's high chair that could be converted into a rocking chair to hold two small children.

John H., as he was known to distinguish him from his father John, chose to settle in what is now the Highlands district, approximately a mile north of the present Langford boundary. They stayed with Elizabeth's parents until the two-storey house was ready at Long Lake. It was reached by steep narrow trails through the woods and over the rocky hills between the Langford plains and the Highland district. Unlike Captain Langford two decades earlier, John H. had no workforce of local Indians and Hawaiian Kanakas, nor a crew of labourers brought from England – he and his father-in-law built the large two-storey lakeshore house in two months in the autumn of 1874.

The family lived on sales of produce, including butter, cheese, eggs, raspberries, black currants and even wild strawberries from Scafe Hill. They kept hens, turkeys, horses, and always a cow or two. There was a huge outdoor Dutch oven for baking bread, 14 loaves at a time. Elizabeth was responsible for much of the dairy produce and the eggs almost until her death in November, 1889, at the age of 42 – only five days after the birth of a stillborn son, her tenth child. The

The John H. Scafe house, shown as it neared completion in the winter of 1874, was built of Douglas fir logs from trees cut near Long Lake. It had a "tremendously large" living room with a huge fireplace. At one end there was a large dining area with an immense table where the children did their lessons. The kitchen was at the other end. All sleeping quarters were upstairs, with no extra heating, but the house was so soundly built the fireplace kept it warm through most winters. No expense was spared for the luxury of glass for the windows. The barely visible figures in the old photograph are John Scafe, son William, daughters Charlotte and Mary Isabel, wife Elizabeth and her parents, Donald and Ann McKenzie (Scafe/Wale collection)

John H. Scafe, seated right, died shortly after this photograph was taken in 1897. Standing behind him are daughters Charlotte (Lottie), Christina (Tena), son James, and daughter Eliza Jane (Jennie). George Wood, Charlotte's husband, and Thomas Scafe are seated with John H. Donald is on the floor in front. William was away, working on a house in Comox. (Scafe/Wale collection)

Three Scafe daughters as young girls, Tina, Jennie and Lottie with their friend Elizabeth Pike, left.
(Scafe/Wale collection)

eldest son William, then 19, made a casket of rough cedar lumber for his mother's burial.

The versatile John H. also made quality kitchen and garden furniture of wicker from willow saplings or dried alder. Customers for his desks, picture frames and baskets included well-known Victorians like Roderick Finlayson, Mr. Trounce of Trounce Alley, and Maynard the photographer.

A surprising source of income was the laundry business. John H. successfully applied for the contract to provide laundry service for the Royal Navy hospital. He traveled over the steep rough Highland roads, through Langford to the Esquimalt naval base, delivering the clean linens in the laundry cart pulled by a team of horses. Then back they came with another load of sheets and blankets to be cleaned and ironed in the steam apparatus designed and built by John H., a certified steam engineer, according to his granddaughter. Hazel lived at the house as a small child and remembered the extraordinary operation in the Highlands:

"The smell of the dirty laundry, heat and steam, camphor and carbolic derived from coal tar, disinfectants and caustic sodas, still haunts me. My aunts feeding sheets and blankets into machines through the steaming rollers, the whirr of other machinery penetrated my ears and drowned out voices. It is still a vivid memory … being bedded down in the rear of the wagon drawn by those two huge lumbering horses on the way to pick up or deliver laundry – the darkness of the night, fear of grotesque shadows and reflections cast by the flickering light of the two coal oil lanterns hanging on either side of the wagon."

After John H. died in 1897 his son William carried on the laundry business with his young wife Alice Wale, his sisters and brothers-in-law. James, a younger brother who died of typhoid in 1900 at the age of 19, is thought to have been a victim of this occupational hazard. He helped with the laundry and handled bedding and clothing picked up at the naval hospital where typhoid was a common disease. The little girls, Hazel and her sister Gertrude, were lucky not to be infected during their frequent trips in the wagon as their father drove back and forth with the laundry.

Nearly 100 years after the family moved into the house in the Highlands, Hazel went back to the site of grandfather Scafe's farm, where her father William grew up and she spent the first few years of her childhood. The three and a half mile drive from her home in Langford with her father and her sister Gertrude, driven by her son Almer Olson, was something of an expedition even in 1970.

"I have heard of Highland District roads 'taking their old-fashioned time' and I must certainly agree with such an apt description. Slowly we wound our way, up and down that meandering violent adversary called a road, growing ever narrower it seemed, until the brush scraped the sides of our car. Past a sign designating Prior Lake

> *"The smell of the dirty laundry, heat and steam, camphor and carbolic derived from coal tar, disinfectants and caustic sodas, still haunts me."*

William Scafe as a young hunter

on the left, and onward we made our way, dodging ruts and protruding jagged rocks. In spite of the minor obstacles of dusty roads, and the all-encompassing density of the forest surrounding us, we made our way along this so-called road, which had now grown gradually steeper with each writhing twist and turn. Visibility was extremely limited at times, barely more than a few feet in some spots. Such was the condition of Highland Road as we encountered it, even in this day and age.

"Patches of what were probably small swampy fields could be seen through tiny openings here and there, between the dense underbrush lining the roadsides to a height of ten to twelve feet. These semi clearings, bordered by scrub willows and low lying salal and wild rose bushes appeared to have been trimmed back in an endeavor to keep the wilderness from taking complete possession of once-cultivated pastureland."

When they turned off the road at the site of the old family home Hazel looked at the rocky knoll with nostalgia.

"No sign of house, barn or woodshed. Long after I had lived there, the farmhouse had burned down, just as the laundry had, years before. Nearby we observed a group of neatly constructed homes with stone fences and several small cedar trees planted out front. Bits of the original wire fencing, fastened to large stumps, were still visible in places, though the whole atmosphere seemed in such contrast with the plantings surrounding the homes, dominating the landscape, mocking the natural forest growth that surrounds the area. … I [remembered] the vastness, the loneliness, the peaceful stillness of yesteryear that had encompassed the old home and still had so much charm for me."

But practicalities overcame nostalgia as Hazel also remembered the disadvantages: daily trips by the younger Scafe children along the jungle-like trail through the woods to the first Highland School, built in 1890; the distance to be trudged on foot to pick up the mail; trips late at night to and from Colwood Farm. Hazel tried to picture her grandfather as a young man and found it hard to understand how "an educated, intellectual man, possessed with reasonable wealth by the standards of the day [could choose] such a remote, rugged place to provide for him the ultimate refuge, happiness and a substantial living."

Long after I had lived there, the farmhouse had burned down, just as the laundry had, years before.

Although the original Scafe farm site is a mile northeast of the present Langford border, Hazel's family stories exemplify what many rural pioneer families endured in the 19th century.

WILLIAM SCAFE AND ALICE WALE

The Wale family was living in the new Colwood farm house when two daughters were married October 19, 1898. The reception for both couples was held in the original 1850s house, in what Hazel remembered as "the ballroom," a much larger room than the smaller parlour of the new building. It must have been Langford's social event of the year. (It is unlikely that Captain Langford and his family referred to their drawing room as a ballroom, but it would have been an impressively large room for the entertainments for which Edward and Flora Langford were well known.)

William and Alice moved into the Scafe House in the Highlands when they were first married and stayed there for three difficult years. The household consisted of William's two sisters and their husbands, the younger children – and the laundry business. Gentle Alice could not have been happy those first years in the old house. Finally her father William Wale, possibly prodded by Ann, took things in hand. Grievances were sorted, it was agreed that all those grown women living in one crowded house could not be expected to continue amicably. Other accommodation was found, but not until after two daughters, Hazel and Gertrude, were born to William and Alice Scafe.

In 1902 William sensibly moved the laundry business to Esquimalt, close to the naval base. He and Alice and their young daughters finally had a home of their own. Alice's mother bought the property for them, William built a little house with the help of his brothers Donald and Thomas. The laundry was housed in a building at the back where Chinese workers assisted, and a Mrs. James worked the charcoal-burning steam irons. The income was never enough to support a growing family. Two more daughters, Winifred and Genevieve, and a son Robert were born there. William found extra work using his carpentry skills at Hatley Park, the spectacular Dunsmuir mansion in Colwood, and other new buildings.

The laundry was housed in a building at the back where Chinese workers assisted...

Arthur is best known as the proprietor of one of Langford's first public transportation companies, the Veteran Stages

The marriage of John H. Scafe's eldest son William to Alice, daughter of William J. Wale and Ann McHugh Wale of Colwood Farm, united two pioneer families who have lived in Langford for more than a century. Alice Maud Mary Wale wore a fashionable gown with a high lace collar, leg-o-mutton sleeves, and a gored skirt with a long flowing veil trimmed with silk orange blossoms. The groom was equally well turned out in a black frock coat with velvet collar and all the other fashionable accessories of the time. Most noticeable was his distinctive moustache. The bride's sister, Daisy Viola Marguerite Wale, was her attendant and John Gedes Fraser was groomsman. Bishop Christie officiated at the wedding in St Andrew's Roman Catholic Cathedral. (Scafe/Wale collection)

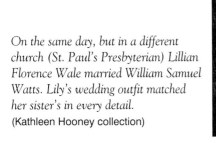

On the same day, but in a different church (St. Paul's Presbyterian) Lillian Florence Wale married William Samuel Watts. Lily's wedding outfit matched her sister's in every detail.
(Kathleen Hooney collection)

The laundry business came to an abrupt end in 1910 when the Royal Navy left Esquimalt, leaving the Pacific base in Canada's hands. Since Canada didn't have a navy, there was no laundry business. The family moved to Tacoma, Washington, for a few years but returned to Langford in 1913. They lived for a while at the 'Lindsey Place' on Millstream Road, then on their property on Goldstream Avenue, now part of the Westbrook Mall.

Members of the Scafe and Wale families remained in the district for many years. William and Ann Wale's son Albert remained in the house on the original Colwood Farm property until his death in 1951. Another son, Arthur, is best known as the proprietor of one of Langford's first public transportation companies, the Veteran Stages, which he founded with Stan Turner. Lillian and Samuel Watts lived on Atkins Road near the railway, for which Mr. Watts worked.

There was more to William and Alice Scafe's lives than laundering, farming and logging. As a young man in 1894 William was persuaded by his friends Henry and Charles Pike to sign on as a crew member on a sealing expedition. The voyage on the schooner Sadie Turpel in 1894 to the Bering Strait, then Tokyo and Yokohama was remembered for grim rations and violent storms. He apprenticed to well-known building contractor John Dean to learn more advanced construction techniques. His experience led to construction jobs at Hatley Park, the Canadian Industries Limited dynamite plant on James Island and other projects. William was also a volunteer in the one of the earliest militia units in the west, the 5th BC Regiment of Garrison Artillery. He attended many training camps at Macaulay Point and became a crack shot. He volunteered for the Boer War, but so many men wanted to join up only a few were taken.

Alice Maude Mary Wale was born in a log house at Elk Lake in 1878 and lived with her parents in the original Langford farm house during the 1890s before her marriage. "She was a petite woman," her granddaughter Hazel remembered, "... weighing less than 98 pounds. Her long hair reached almost to her knees as she combed her long tresses over and over in front of her unusual square looking glass. She wore it piled high, coiled in a bun on top of her head, or combed and plaited then wrapped in coils at the nape of her neck. [She] never used cosmetics but kept scrupulously clean thanks to Sunlight laundry soap and warm water for the greater part of her lifetime." This dainty lady, who was thought of as "like royalty," was also a competent self-taught veterinarian, mid-wife to farm animals, and mother of six: Hazel, Gertrude, Katherine, Genevieve, Robert and David. She was also a crack shot in defense of her chickens and geese that were constantly in danger from marauding raccoons and mink from the banks of Mill Stream.

Several of the Scafe and Wale descendants who still live in Langford appear in later chapters.

This dainty lady, who was thought of as "like royalty," was also a competent self-taught veterinarian...

She was also a crack shot in defense of her chickens and geese that were constantly in danger from marauding raccoons and mink from the banks of Mill Stream.

Section II

Langford's Communities

Until the late 20th century Langford and its western neighbours beyond Parson's Bridge were all part of Esquimalt District. They were unorganized territories under Provincial Government jurisdiction without local government. When the Capital Regional District was formed Langford, Colwood, View Royal, Metchosin and Sooke each had one director on the CRD board, thoroughly outnumbered by multiple directors from Victoria and the more populated municipalities.

Finally a higher level of government brought incorporation and self-government to the District of Langford. Boundaries were drawn, zigzagging for reasons now forgotten, between Langford and its neighbours. Within this oddly shaped area of 10,245 acres are several distinct communities brought together to make a viable town in 1992. The original village in the Millstream/Goldstream area including Florence Lake; Happy Valley/Luxton, and Goldstream/The Malahat are the earliest communities.

Goldstream Avenue in the 1950s with the Langford Plains building in the distance behind the automobile, had not changed much since the years between the wars. This rural road was still part of the Island Highway when this picture was taken in 1954. (Myrna Harling Photo)

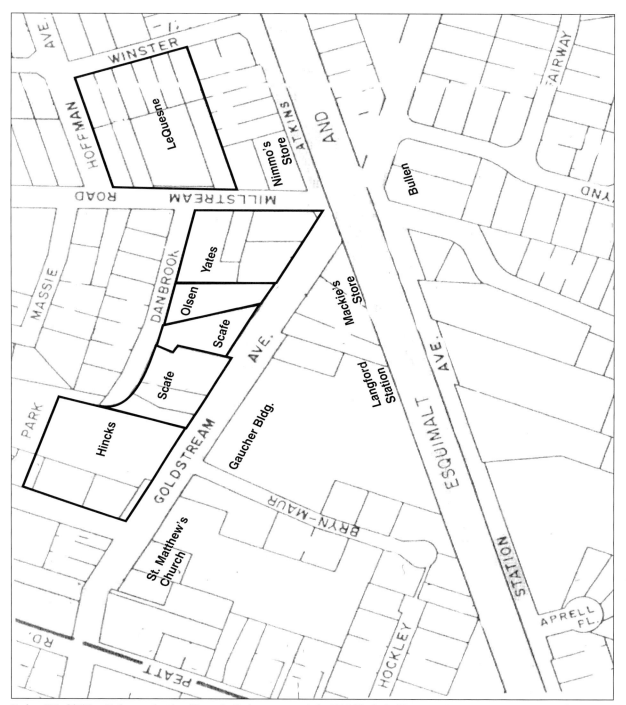

Before World War II the north side of Langford's 'main street,' the 700 block Goldstream Avenue, was a mixture of residential and business activity between the Yates family's old stone house on Millstream Road and the Hincks farm at Claude Road. Between them were the Scafes and Olsons and their sawmill. It is now the Westbrook shopping plaza, a credit union and a service station. The western communities RCMP headquarters, shops and a large restaurant now cover the LeQuesne property. (Section of 1920s map donated by Jean Strachan)

7

LANGFORD VILLAGE

By 1912 the narrow unpaved road west from Millstream Road was emerging as Langford's first 'commercial' centre, with its railway station, two general stores and a two-storey multi-use building fondly remembered by generations as the Gaucher Building, a Langford landmark until 1972. The dirt road that was part of the highway is now an attractive divided boulevard known as the 700 block Goldstream Avenue.

The history of Goldstream Avenue and Millstream Road which recently became the Veterans Memorial Parkway, is divided into three sections, each illustrating an era of Langford's diverse past with photographs and family stories.

BEFORE WORLD WAR I

The Langford Cash Store which opened beside the E&N railway station in 1904 was the first general store. A few years later, in 1911, Ernest Gaucher built his two-story frame building for his many enterprises.

Mr. Gaucher came to Canada from Manchester in 1908. He intended to build greenhouses to start a nursery business, but according to his daughter, the late Marion Pitt, "a great snow storm knocked the greenhouses flat, so he went into other businesses." His later Langford enterprises included an automobile garage, the first movie theatre in Langford, and a popular dance hall on the upper floor of his building. He and his wife and daughters lived in a house on the east side of the building and his sister, Mrs. Whitfield, lived on the other side near the present Bryn Maur Road.

In an interview shortly before she died Marion Gaucher Pitt talked about her father's family. "It was a big step from the family business in Manchester, a butcher shop famous for its sausages and Melton Mowbray pies. I remember a photograph of the English shop showing a staff of 20 under a sign proclaiming 'By Appointment' to a

His later Langford enterprises included an automobile garage, the first movie theatre in Langford, and a popular dance hall on the upper floor of his building.

The Gaucher building in the 700 block of Goldstream Road had many incarnations from its construction in 1911 to its fiery end in 1972. (Wallace Klages photo, courtesy Myrna Harling)

royal personage." Mr. Gaucher later operated a garage and gas station at the corner of Goldstream Road and the Island Highway where Marion is remembered as the only female gas attendant in the area at the time. There the family lived at the back and also ran a tea room. In his later years Ernest Gaucher lived with his son-in-law and daughter, Fred and Marion Pitt, on a 12-acre property at the end of Esquimalt Harbour between the Six Mile House and the Canadian National railway tracks. "Dad still made excellent pies and sausages and supplied some of the best hotels including the Empress. The Melton Mowbray pies were as big as dinner plates," Marion recalled. "I used to help him stuff sausages into their casings so I'm still not much of a sausage lover" she admitted in an interview when she was in her eighties.

Marion is remembered as the only female gas attendant in the area at the time.

The Gaucher building in 1952 after renovations by Homer and Elizabeth Barker, with their daughter Myrna's beauty salon and flats upstairs. (Myrna Harling photo)

Hazel Scafe Olson remembered the dance hall around 1915 as "the liveliest place around … musicians played, dancers danced and the building literally swayed back and forth. [Mr. Gaucher] was so alarmed he installed several huge angle braces at the rear, adding supports to the floor for safety. Over the years it was also a meeting place for various organizations. My brother-in-law Vollie McTavish and his son Arthur often volunteered to transport chairs to the hall and return them the following day. Until it burned down in 1972 the building offered a great deal to the small community of Langford, providing entertainment, housing and employment to hundreds of local persons."

The fire at 6 a.m. on April 22, 1972, which ended the Gaucher building's long and useful life. (Langford Fire Department Photo)

Well known Victoria dance teacher Florence Clough Drummond also remembers dances at Mr. Gaucher's hall. Part of her childhood was spent with her parents at the home her grandfather, Henry Greenwood, who lived near the railway station on property that he later sold to the Royal Colwood Golf Club.

When Florence was about 10 years old her mother took her to one of the dances at the hall where Madame Valda gave ballroom dancing lessons. Few people knew at the time that Madame Valda was a highly trained classical dancer who had been a member of the Paris Opera ballet company. Florence was invited to visit the little house at Luxton where the dancer and her husband lived, and was shown a trunk full of treasured ballet shoes and costumes. Valda told Florence stories of her life with ballet companies, including Pavlova's famous touring company. The little girl was enchanted.

Madame Valda was a highly trained classical dancer who had been a member of the Paris Opera ballet company.

Miss Clough gave a dancing exhibition at a dance at Langford Lakeside sponsored by the Victoria Girls' Band...

Florence recalls that another French lady, a Mrs. Hill whose husband was a solicitor for the Dunsmuirs, helped Madame Valda start a dance studio in Victoria, over a shop at 1208 Government Street. Florence eagerly attended ballet classes and began teaching beginners when she was 16. She traveled to the U.S. to study and returned to open her own dance studio, where she taught for nearly 50 years.

A 1931 newspaper clipping notes that Miss Clough gave a dancing exhibition at a dance at Langford Lakeside sponsored by the Victoria Girls' Band, where streamers, paper hats and confetti "contributed to the carnival spirit." Rosemary (Bullen) Brimacombe also remembers that Miss Clough brought large groups of her dance pupils on the train for picnics at Langford.

Madame Valda, the tiny ballet dancer from Luxton by way of Paris, and Florence Clough Drummond both contributed to Langford's early entertainments.

Two general stores supplied groceries and feed for the small population on Goldstream and Millstream roads before World War I.

A second general store was opened in 1912 by John C. Thom, who sold it later to Mr. and Mrs. L. G. Wilkinson. The two-storey building stood beside the railway tracks near the intersection of Atkins Road, Millstream Road and the Highway near the railway's level crossing. Mr. J. C. Nimmo owned and operated the business until he sold it to Cyril and Lillian Price in 1949.

First known photograph of the Langford Cash Store was built beside the railway station in 1904 by L. G. Scott for Wilson and Gene Taylor. Lumber for the $600 building came by rail from a Shawnigan Lake mill.
(Rod Bayles photo)

Genevieve Scafe, later Mrs. Vollie McTavish, with McTavish's smart two-seater Dodge, on the recently paved Island Highway in the early 1920s. (Scafe/Wale photo)

BETWEEN THE WARS - 1919 TO 1939

This is the period that children who lived in Langford in the 1920s and '30s remember. The stories and photographs supplied by several families provide a 'virtual tour' of this extraordinary mix of log cottages and stone houses, English flower gardens and cow pastures, poultry farms and sawmills, an automobile garage, tennis courts and a country church.

If you had arrived from the city by automobile in the late 1920s or early 1930s you would have come along the Old Island Highway past Parson's Bridge, up the hill to the right turn on the part of the

Lillian (Wale) Watt at the railway cottage on Atkins Road. Her husband Samuel was a foreman with the E. & N. Railway (Kathleen Hooney collection)

Members of the prestigious Colwood Golf Club, where the Prince of Wales, later Edward VIII, played during several visits to Victoria, gathered for this photograph in front of the 1921 clubhouse. Joseph Sayward, one of the club's founders and a major financial backer, is standing centre rear with Mrs. Sayward at his left. (BC Archives D-05176)

Genevieve Scafe and her sister Winifred worked as waitresses in the dining room of the Colwood Golf Club along with other local girls, including Mary McTavish, Christina Brotherston and Thelma Brotherston. Genevieve, second from right, was employed as a cook and later given charge of the dining room for several years. When the Prince of Wales was there in 1919 the club professional presented the ball he played with that day to Genevieve.

(Scafe/Wale photo)

highway now called Goldstream Avenue. This is the same route Captain Langford marked for improvements when he was a road commissioner for Governor Douglas in the 1850s. His original house is gone but at the time of this 'tour' Albert Wale would still be living in the second house on the same site. On the south side of the Highway the Colwood Golf Club (not yet 'Royal') had beautified the former sheep pastures, leaving a row of trees lining the road.

On your right, opposite the golf course, as you drove along in an open car, you might have been aware of a piggery, said to have been located on the site of the present St. Anthony's Medical Clinic. Other sources claim there was also a poultry farm nearby.

If you had taken the E. & N. train from Victoria instead of coming by car, you would have approached Langford near Atkins Road, past the railway spur that used to go to the Atkins brothers lime quarry at the foot of Mill Hill.

As the train slowed down before the level crossing you would have seen a small stone house across Atkins Road, and behind that on Millstream Road the brown shingled home of one of Langford's best known families, the LeQuesnes.

Ritchie LeQuesne wrote a brief history of his family from the time his grandparents, Frank and Annie LeQuesne, came to Langford in 1922 and bought the Langford Garage from Mr. Goucher in 1923. Their sons, Ernest and Bert, came from Kelowna to help run the business.

The LeQuesne home from 1925 to 1946, surrounded by land extending from Millstream east to Winster Road, and north to Hoffman. Kitty LeQuesne is shown with two of her three sons.
(La Quesne family photo)

Ernest LeQuesne, soldier, businessman and sportsman.
(LeQuesne family photo)

In 1925 Ernest returned to Kelowna to marry Catherine (Kitty) Ritchie. They bought the house on Millstream Road next to the present RCMP western communities headquarters. Their three sons, Jack, Ritchie and Alan were born and raised there. The LeQuesne family sold the Gaucher building and built a new larger garage and gas station at Colwood Corners in 1931. In 1940 Ernest, a veteran of the First World War, was called back into the army as an instructor at the Officers' Training Centre in Gordon Head. Bert continued to run the business until 1945 when it was sold to Union Oil Co. Ernest and Kitty LeQuesne bought the Mackie store and living quarters when Ernest returned from World War II service. They sold it in 1948 and moved to a house on Langford Lake at 2914 Leigh Road. Ernest worked at Mac and Mac, a hardware and automotive supply business on Government Street in Victoria until his sudden death in 1957. Kitty stayed in the Leigh Road home until 1983 when she moved to the Priory Hospital. She died there suddenly in 1987. All three sons and many grandchildren and great grandchildren still live in the Langford area.

Bert LeQuesne married Dora Wilkie in 1939. Dora was one of the first district nurses in the western communities, driving as far as Metchosin and Sooke on her rounds. Bert died in 1955, but Dora and her younger son Robert still live in Esquimalt (2002).

The virtual tour by train would continue across the level crossing to Langford Station (formerly Colwood Station) on the aptly named

In this 1920 photo from the Bayles family collection the general store has a gasoline pump and a sign across the foundation advertising Everybody Smokes Chum Tobacco. (See Mackie biography in section on Langford branch of Canadian Legion, page 156.)

Station Road which runs parallel to the Highway/Goldstream Avenue. Passengers got off at the back of the building first known as the Langford Cash Store, with its feed sheds at the back.

The Langford Cash Store became A. G. Mackie, Groceries and Feed after World War I when Sergeant Major Alex Mackie bought the store from James Mellis in 1919. Mr. Mellis sold the Mackies his stock of groceries and arranged to have his postal contract turned over to the new owner, who served as Langford Station postmaster from 1919 to 1945.

The Mackies "had the somewhat dubious distinction of being the first operators of slot machines in the district," Hazel Olson wrote in her memoirs. "For a short time it was a source of extra income, until school children, the majority customers, discovered the trick of lifting a corner of the machine. Their winnings soared, the Mackies checked the constant ringing of bells and jingling of nickels, and adjustments were made. Profits diminished and the slot machines were removed"

Across the Highway from the station, the virtual traveller would have seen a large stone house, the home of prominent Victoria lawyer James Stuart Yates and his wife, Annie (Austin) Yates.

Mr. and Mrs. Yates were both born in Victoria, James Stuart in 1857, the son of James and Mary Yates, and Annie, daughter of John Joel and Sarah Austin, in 1869. The younger James was educated in Scotland and received his law degree at the University of Edinburgh. Annie was educated at Craigflower School and St. Ann's Academy. They were married in 1891 and lived on his father's 400 acre estate on the Gorge until it was subdivided in 1908. After a few years in a house in the city on Elford Street they moved to their preferred

Mr. and Mrs. James Stuart Yates and their sons Robert, Harry and Austin, 1930s. (Yates family collection, Robert Fort photo)

Guests at James Yates's 80th birthday party in 1937 included many lawyers, celebrating the long career of their senior colleague who had been practicing law in Victoria since 1883. He was still commuting to his office in the Central Building in the 1940s, in partnership with his youngest son Robert. (Robert Fort Photos, Yates family collection)

country life in Langford with flower gardens, large oak trees and a carpet of wildflowers in spring. The back driveway led to the cow barn and paddock where their popular Chinese dairy man, Moo or Low Ma, looked after at least one cow. Annie's niece, Nell Willson, lived with them until she married in the late 1930s. Austin Yates, the eldest son, and his wife Maude also stayed with his parents during the 1920s on their return from England, then moved to a house on Dunford Road. Their daughters Adela and Margaret attended Langford School. Austin and Maude lived in the stone house in the 1950s after his parents died. The property is now a service station and convenience store.

1952: Austin Yates donated the land at the western corner of the family property for a firehall in memory of his parents, Mr. and Mrs. James Stuart Yates. The 1952 building replaced a totally inadequate garage in the basement of the community hall farther along Goldstream Avenue. (Langford Fire Department photo)

2001: One large oak tree survives beside the much-changed Langford fire hall, built on land donated by the Yates family in 1952. An undistinguished L-shaped office building and parking lot cover the site of the house and the lawn which once served as a tennis court. The photo was taken from the site of the 1930 Olson sawmill. (M. Duffus photo)

A Digression:

The ladies in the garden party photograph (following page) and their friends are mentioned often in Victoria newspapers from the 1920s and 1930s. Two industrious correspondents, thought to be Nora Hincks and Doris Bayles, supplied Victoria newspapers with accounts of the social life and volunteer activities of Langford residents even in the depth of the great depression of the 1930s. Many of the families mentioned lived along the section of the Old Island Highway that is now Langford's business centre, between Millstream and Peatt roads. These are some excerpts from Bonnie Josephson's collection of newspaper clippings.

June 14, 1922, the Langford Women's Auxiliary met at the home of Mrs. Eldridge to complete arrangements for a garden fete on July 1 at the residence of Mr. and Mrs. Douglas Bullen, Station Road. Home produce, needlework, candy and talent stalls were to be represented by Canada, England, Scotland and Ireland. Attractions included afternoon tea, ice cream, dancing by Madam Valda's pupils, Maypole dance, comic baseball, clock golf, nail driving and coconut shies.

In September that year the social news consisted of the departures of a number of summer residents from their Langford lake cottages: Mr. and Mrs. C. Bosustow and their daughter Roberta;

Attractions included afternoon tea, ice cream, dancing by Madam Valda's pupils, Maypole dance

Ladies of Langford with friends and children were photographed in front of the large oak tree in the Yates garden for at a special occasion garden party in the late 20s or early 30s. The gentleman at the back is the minister of St. Matthew's Church, Mr. Atheson-Lyle. Miss Lillian Savory is the tiny lady at his left shoulder. To her left is Mrs. Ritchie behind her daughter Kitty LeQuesne. Annie Yates is the other small woman without a hat back row centre. Third and fourth from the left in the back row are Mrs. Heggie and Mrs. Bennett. Mrs. Austin Yates is seated at right, and her daughter Adela is the young girl in the print dress seated, centre, with Mrs. Goodmanson and Eileen Hincks to her right behind the black and white dog. Others in the picture are Mrs. William Whitney-Griffiths with her young son, Mrs. Reynolds, Mrs. Staverman, Sheila Pennington and Doris Bayles. (Robert Fort photo, from Adela (Yates) Abel)

Mr. and Mrs. H. A. Davies; Mr. and Mrs. Walter Luney and the Misses Edna and Eleanor Luney, Mr. and Mrs. H. L. Butteris and their three children, and Alderman and Mrs. James Adam and family.

A 1927 article, *Women to Help Building of Hall,* reported on the formation of the Women's Auxiliary to the Prince Edward Branch, No. 91, of the Canadian Legion. The meeting was held at "The Gowans," the home of Mrs. A. G. Mackie. Mrs. H. C. Bennett was elected president pro tem and others officers were Mrs. Mackie and Mrs. George Cooney. Mrs. Mackie explained the purpose of the auxiliary was to assist in raising funds for building the branch hall, and the need to support the masquerade ball on November 4. At the close of the meeting the hostess served tea.

Social notes in 1927 included the news that Mrs. Earle was the guest of Mrs. Hasenfratz at Deer Lodge, Langford Lake. Guests at a Colwood Women's Institute meeting included Mrs. Cowie, Miss Lillian Savory, Mrs. L. G. Wilkinson, Mrs. H. A. Hincks and Miss M. Aikman. There was a bridal shower at the Tom Thumb Tea Rooms for Mr. and Mrs. Thomas Seward, nee Kathleen Gaucher.

Mrs. H. C. Bennett and Mrs. H. A. Hincks were joint hostesses at a delightful children's "corn" party held on the beach at Langford Lakeside. Games, boating and other attractions were thoroughly enjoyed by the youthful guests, but the main feature of the afternoon was a huge bonfire on which the corn was cooked. Guests included Betty; Margaret and Glenys Smedley, Cecily and Pamela Bennett, Stella and Eileen Hincks, Elizabeth and Norton Welch, Jack Wilkinson, Keith and Campbell Brown, Dean Johnston, Rodney Bayles, Howard Smedley, Kenneth Hincks and Henry Bennett. Another noteworthy children's party was held at "Mabville" on Millstream road. Hostess Mrs. J. T. Jalland was assisted by Mrs. W. Bradley and Mrs. Austin Yates.

Results of tennis tournaments were reported, along with names of club ladies who served tea at the Saturday and Sunday games on the board courts. Harvest festival decorations at St Matthew's Church were described at length and house guests were noted. Girl Guides who passed various tests were listed, including Esther and Kathleen Hutchinson, Shirley Rant, Adela Yates, Fairy Welch and Elsie Smith. Lord and Lady Baden Powell, founder of The Scout and Guide movements, even paid a short visit to the Langford Scouts.

Continuing the virtual tour along the north side of Goldstream, you would come to Hazel and Axel Olson's house on property they

Mrs. Earle was the guest of Mrs. Hasenfratz at Deer Lodge, Langford Lake.

Mrs. H. C. Bennett and Mrs. H. A. Hincks were joint hostesses at a delightful children's "corn" party held on the beach at Langford Lakeside

Axel Olson built this sawmill beside the Olson house in 1930 to provide cedar and fir lath for plastering contractors. Hills of sawdust provided a bike riding challenge for young boys, but neighbours were not pleased when the mill was built. (Scafe/Wale photo)

Hazel and Axel Olson were married in 1919. (Scafe/Wale photo).

bought from Hazel's parents, William and Alice Scafe, shortly before their marriage in 1919. After years of moving back and forth to various houses on Millstream Road William and Alice bought the property that covered the central part of what is now the Westbrook Plaza.

With the time machine still set for the twenties and thirties, the tour would pass William and Alice Scafe's house on the way to the Hincks property next door. After serving with the British Army in the Boer War Harold Hincks travelled to the United States and Canada, then returned to England to marry. In 1912 he and his bride Nora settled in Langford at the west end of the present Westbrook

William and Alice Scafe, left, with their daughter Hazel Olson and her son Almer beside a truck load of cordwood ready for delivery in 1922. (Scafe/Wale photo)

Centre. Their house, *Holmwood,* was originally built in 1903 by the Frewing brothers then enlarged in 1908. Income from the huge vegetable garden, fruit trees, berries, magnificent holly trees and a herd of dairy cows supplemented profits from a large chicken ranch operation. At one point, according to notes attributed to their son Kenneth, they had 2000 free-range chickens. They also shipped day-old leghorn chicks all over the province, and Ken Hincks recalled a parade float promoting **Langford – the Egg Capital of B.C.** The business continued until the late1930s.

The younger sons, Oswald and Claude, and Almer Olson were school friends. Hazel Olson remembered her son bringing home the day's supply of skim milk or buttermilk from the Hincks dairy when it cost two cents a quart. Claude was killed in World War II but his name lives on in the road named in his honour. Mrs. Hincks took great interest in St. Matthew's Church activities and community affairs. She is especially remembered for her fund-raising teas and garden parties, and her superb floral arrangements with a wide variety of blooms from her own garden. Newspaper clippings record the many prizes she won at flower shows and fairs. Her son Kenneth followed her as exhibitor and winner of countless trophies and awards for produce at local exhibitions.

Harold and Nora Hincks added to a log cabin originally built earlier in the century. (Hincks family photo)

A herd of dairy cows once grazed on the Hincks property on Goldstream Avenue near Claude Road, now the western end of the Westbrook Plaza. A profitable chicken ranch on another part of the land supplied chickens to many parts of the province. The vegetable and flower gardens, heavily fortified with readily available manure, were the envy of all the neighbours.
(Hincks family photos)

Doris Bayles was born in Cairo where her father was head of the Thomas Cook and Sons travel office. She married a World War I veteran and moved to Canada with him. He died the following year but she was determined never to go back to England, preferring to live in a tiny cottage next to the Hincks' home. Her neighbour across the road was Grace Brown, whose brother, Bert Bayles, helped the young widow with chores and repairs. Bert and Doris were the first couple married when St. Matthew's Church was completed in 1924.

Bert and Doris Bayles built their house near the Langford Plains building. It was modified almost beyond recognition in the 1990s to become the Water Wheel Pub.
(Rod Bayles Family Photo)

Rod Bayles' aunt and uncle, the Browns, lived in this house near St. Matthew's Church.
(Bayles family photo)

A visitor in the 1920s could walk farther west along the highway to Langford Elementary School and the homes of a several more families, including the Jacksons whose son Stan was a well-known basketball player with the Dominos team. Jack Douglas, a grandson of Sir James Douglas, his wife, Orsa Chungrannes, and their daughter, Orsa Marie, lived on the south side of the highway near the school. The cluster of houses gave way to an almost uninhabited stretch of road until the post World War II development began. The pre-war walking tour would continue back toward the station on the south side of the Highway.

St. Matthew's Church was a small brown-shingled country church. It was built in 1924 and demolished in 1972. Records of the parish building committee show that the Hudson's Bay Company contributed $500 towards its construction, and a cash book shows a donation of $300 from Mrs. James Dunsmuir of Hatley Park. Total building cost was $1,963.75. Newspaper clippings from the 1920s report teas, fundraising, flower shows and other activities arranged by the Ladies' Guild. The building stood near the road at the front of a square that now includes a popular restaurant, a movie theatre, a thrift shop and the local newspaper office.

On the same side as St. Matthew's, Mrs. Whitfield's house, the Gaucher building and the Gaucher's family home were side by side east of Bryn Maur Road.

The LeQuesne Garage operated in the Gaucher building between 1923, when Frank and Annie LeQuesne bought the building, to 1931. Early meetings of the Prince Edward Branch of the Canadian Legion were held in the upper room. The Belmont Dramatic Club also met and performed there in the 1930s.
(Metchosin School Museum Photo)

Marshwood was built by Henry Greenwood and sold to John and Cecilia Bullen who moved to Langford for a quiet country life. They raised chickens like many of their neighbours, and one Victoria directory lists the property as a 'rabbitry.'
(Metchosin School Museum photo)

Walking back to the train station the visitor would come to *Marshwood*, likely the grandest house in all of Langford. It was built by Henry Greenwood, a retired landowner, who sold it in 1920 to John Douglas Fitzherbert Bullen and his wife Cecilia, descendants of the Douglas and Helmcken families. The garden was the scene of many church teas and other neighbourhood gatherings. Mr. Bullen was instrumental in organizing the first Langford Boy Scout Troop, along with Allen Bodman, Captain Wagner and others with a mili-

A load of telephone poles ready for transport by train from Langford Station in 1929. The picture was taken behind Mackie's general store looking east toward Colwood. The straight stretch of tracks running parallel to Station Road is said to have been used by the RCAF pilots-in-training for 'bombing' practice during World War II: planes from the Patricia Bay air field flew low along the tracks, aiming sacks of flour at trains along the route, according to the story.
(Goldstream Museum Photo)

tary background. A large unused building at the rear of the property was remodeled for the scout hall and a cub group as well. Mrs.Bullen was an active member of the Guild of St. Matthews Church and president of the Langford Women's Institute for 20 years.

The visitor's virtual tour would end back at the train station, after an afternoon of hospitality from any or all of the local families or, if it happened to be a weekend in June, 1928, a tennis match at the new wooden courts on property donated by Mr. and Mrs. Hincks.

LANGFORD TENNIS CLUB

The Langford Tennis Club began on two grass courts, one at the Yates home, the other at the Brown's. In 1928 members bought planks from Lemon-Gonnason lumberyard, at as low a cost as could be negotiated, and built two splendid wooden courts on land owned by Harold and Nora Hincks. Other founding members of the club included Ernest and Kitty LeQuesne and Doris and Bert Bayles. James Stuart Yates and Ernie LeQuesne presided and the opening ceremonies in June, 1928. The clubhouse was known as the tea hut where the ladies made tea on a kerosene stove to serve with cookies to players and spectators.

Members were keenly competitive. A tournament in August, 1931, against the James Bay Athletic Association at the JBAA's new courts near the old Gorge Hotel was reported in the Colonist under the heading *Tennis Match at Gorge Quarters ends in Narrow Margin for Visitors.*

Players on opening day, 1928, have been identified by several players who were children at the time. There are differences of opinion, but most agree that the opening day group includes, left to right, Kitty and Ernest LeQuesne, Nell Willson (niece of Mr. and Mrs. Yates), Bert or Ted Bayles, Nora Hincks, possibly Stan Turner, Doris Bayles, unknown. (Photo courtesy Jack LeQuesne)

"Playing under perfect weather conditions and within a setting unequalled on the Pacific coast, as far as the general layout of tennis courts is concerned, the J.B.A.A. over the weekend lost to Langford. … A large gallery followed the games and so keen was the competition that until the final set was played the result was in doubt.

"The Team from the 'Gateway to the Malahat' went home victorious, winning six sets to four. Two hundred and sixteen games in all were played, 111 going to Langford and 105 to the losers."

The courts near Claude Road were in use until after World War II, but had to be resurfaced with tar to cover the galvanized nails that began to pop up dangerously. The club moved to land donated off Orono Road, and now plays on the upper courts at Royal Roads University.

When the Langford School opened in 1914 one of the earliest classes included children of well known families including the Scafe. Marion Gaucher is second from right in the second row. The boy with the hat at the left of the row has been identified as William Gibson, later known throughout Victoria as the photographer who took class pictures at all the schools for many years.
(Scafe/Wale collection)

Well-known Langford families are represented in this 1933 photo of the elementary school, showing a second classroom added at the rear of the original one-room school. They are identified as Lyle Wilkinson, Oswald Hincks, Almer Olson, Robert Simpson, Hazel Baynes, Adela Yates, John Bullen, Ed Wulff, Hamish Bullen, Maurice Buckley and teacher Hilda Buy, back row; Mary Hammill, Margaret Brotherston, Phyllis Wilkinson, Kitty Staverman, Phyllis Moore, Ada Carlow, Alice Tayler, Glenys Smedley, Gladys Staverman, Margaret Yates and Frances Wale, middle row; Henry Bennett, Ronald Dixon, Howard Henn, Rodney Bayles, Jimmy Duncan, Claude Heggie, Billy Ord and Claude Hincks, seated in the front row. (Sid Finch collection)

St. Aidan's prep school for boys occupied this building which still stands on Preston Road behind Ruth King Elementary. Headmaster Ashley Sparks and his family lived in the house at the left of the classrooms and students' dormitory.
(M. Duffus photo)

MILSTREAM ROAD

The winding wagon road of the 1890s when the William Wale children walked to Colwood School from Yew Tree Farm was described by Hazel Scafe Olson from her mother's recollections. Alice (Wale) Scafe remembered the walk home August heat, over the fields and through the woods of the old Langford farm, on constant lookout for the many cattle, wild steers and game that roamed the area. At Goldstream Road they crossed the E. & N. railway tracks and continued up Millstream Road where cougars were quite commonplace and much feared. "The soft powdery hot brown dust along this narrow wagon road that was bordered by wild rose bushes, willows, underbrush and ferns had jagged rock outcroppings, hazards ruinous to the long white cotton stockings worn by the girls" who trudged along in their blue serge dresses and " heavy high-laced

Henry Pike's house was south of the Pond House near Larkhall Road. Emily Carr's friend Humphrey Toms described it as a tidily kept, permanently inhabited house which "goes by the grandiose name of Lark Hall," which may have had something to do with Emily's nickname for her rented house, Rat Hall. (Metchosin School Museum)

shoes with brass caps at the toes and 'blakies' at the heels or soles to keep them from wearing out" on the long walk from Sooke Road.

This section of the road that used to be in sight of the stream that gave it its name is now part of the Veterans Memorial Parkway, a four-lane divided connecting road between the Trans Canada Highway and Sooke Road. The road continues north of the Highway to the Highlands District where it still resembles the narrow wagon road of earlier days.

One of the oldest houses on Millstream Road was the Porter House, later known as the Pond House. It appears to be the house built in the 1850s by James Porter, a workman at Captain Langford's farm. Mr. Porter's daughter Mary, reminiscing in the early 1920s, said her stepmother did laundry for the Langfords while her father built a house for the family on Millstream Road. It was occupied over the years by various families, including William and Ann Wale who are thought to have built the much later house on the property, farther back from the improved gravel road. Florence Lake was a gentle two-mile walk along bush trails for picnics, hunting or fishing before construction of the Trans Canada highway became the great divide. Millstream Road was not entirely a picturesque rural road at the time. Parts of it were line with cordwood piled high along the sides, ready to be picked up for delivery to homes with wood-burning stoves, and to the greenhouses near Florence Lake. Hazel Olson describes the scene:

Mr. Porter's daughter Mary, reminiscing in the early 1920s, said her stepmother did laundry for the Langfords while her father built a house for the family on Millstream Road.

The McTavish truck, Marion Gaucher at right, was typical of the trucks that hauled cordwood for wood-burning stoves.
(Scafe/Wale collection)

The William Wale house on Millstream Road, built near the old Porter House, called the Pond House because of a large swamp or pond near the present Larkhall Road.
(BC Archives F-05886)

"William Wale and others employed Chinese woodcutters for logging activities in the Highland District in the early part of the 20th century. Six or more of them lived in the old house by the pond, presumably the old Porter House, about half a mile south of what is now the Trans Canada Highway. Every evening each man carried home a carefully chosen piece of wood to be split into short lengths to fit the small stove where they cooked their meals of rice, mushrooms and fatty pork dipped from a large community bowl. Saturday nights they walked to town and returned Sunday evenings carrying a sack of rice on one side of their pole and a rock for balance on the other.

"The woodcutters were brought from China by the head man who helped with fares and arranged jobs for a fee. Many were hired by Painter Brothers fuel company, who always had a good relationship with their Chinese employees. They transported thousands of cords of wood on sleds with greased runners, pulled by horses and left in huge stacks of cordwood along the sides of Millstream Road. The stacks lined the roadside as far as a quarter of a mile, and were often nine to 12 feet high. The sleds, owned by the Painters' company, left greasy patches on the bushes alongside the road, coating our clothes as we trudged along the narrow road back and forth from school – shooing away the cattle and sheep which roamed freely in this part of Langford.

"Later the Chinese worked in skid-road logging on Triangle Mountain, where George Woodruff pulled logs down the mountainside with his team of horses. The logs were then loaded onto Vollie McTavish's truck to be taken to the log dump at Parson's Bridge.The white truck, one of the finest vehicles available, also carted wood fuel to Vollie's father's lime kiln at Rosebank, near Fort Rodd Hill, a part of Defense Department land since World War II. (Editor's note: some city directories give names of the Chinese workmen and farmers in Goldstream, Langford and Happy Valley in earlier days, but further information is not so far available.)

The house had a wide verandah where Emily and her maid Blanche took meals cooked on a camp stove constructed under Emily's supervision.

EMILY CARR AT "RAT HALL"

Emily Carr was anxious to go on a sketching trip in the country just two months after her second heart attack in April, 1939. Her friend Humphrey Toms drove her around Langford "in a drizzle" and found what Toms described as "a clean empty shack" for rent for $7.50 a month. According to Hazel Olson's memoirs this was the home built by her grandparents, William and Alice Wale, on the site of the Old Pond House on Millstream Road. They still pastured

Noted Canadian artist Emily Carr rented this house on Millstream Road for a sketching trip in June, 1939. She is pictured with her dogs and her friend Flora Hamilton Burns on the steps of the William Wale House on Millstream Road, June 24, 1939. Hazel Olson's notes confirm the artist stayed in "the house recently completed by the W. J. Wale family."
(BC Archives C-05235)

sheep on the fields, and the pond was home to a colony of frogs. It was about half a mile north of the Goldstream Avenue intersection and only a ten-minute walk to the post office and general store for Emily's maid Blanche.

The house had a wide verandah where Emily and Blanche took meals cooked on a camp stove constructed under Emily's supervision. Her camping experience was vast after years of painting expeditions in her legendary caravan known as The Elephant.

The complete privacy, the views and the flat fields where she could walk outdoors to sketch must have given the 68-year-old artist a feeling of freedom as she recuperated from her hospital stay. Flora Hamilton Burns was one of several friends who visited her and presumably met the family of young rats that gave the house its temporary name. They lived in the field under her window, not in the house, and entertained Emily during her two-week stay. Humphrey Toms suggested that the name was also linked to the next property "permanently inhabited and kept tidily [which] goes by the grandiose name of Lark Hall." Emily's comments on her short visit can be found in letters reprinted in Nan Cheney's book *Dear Nan.*

"...the next property "permanently inhabited and kept tidily [which] goes by the grandiose name of Lark Hall."

Brigadier General John Rockingham, commander of 9th Canadian Infantry (Highland) Brigade, accepts the surrender from German General Ferdinand Heim at Boulogne on September 18, 1944, after the Canadians took the town. John had gone overseas with the Canadian Scottish Regiment as a lieutenant in 1941. In July, 1944, he was promoted to lieutenant colonel and a month later to brigadier in charge of the Canadian troops who took the town. At the end of the war John Rockingham was considered the best fighting brigadier in the Canadian Army, famous for keeping close to his men in a small armoured scout car. Following the war he held management positions with the B.C. Electric Railway Company and Pacific Stage Lines. He rejoined the army to command the 25th Canadian Infantry Brigade in Korea in 1950-52. (The Encyclodpedia of British Columbia). Major General Rockingham, as he became, was born in 1911 and died in Vancouver in 1987. (Photo lent by his sister, Mary Rockingham Hughes)

THE ROCKINGHAM FAMILY

John realized that his father's 300 acres of rock and trees were not suitable for raising sheep.

In a recent interview Mrs. Leslie Hughes told the story of how her parents, Mr. and Mrs. Walter Edward Rockingham, and her younger brother John came to live in Langford in 1929. Walter Rockingham had been general manager of Pacific Cable Board in the West Indies before he retired to Australia. For reasons his daughter Mary finds incomprehensible, he then moved to Vancouver Island and bought "a folly of a sheep farm" on the northern part of Millstream Road. He persuaded his son John to leave a post-high school job at an Australian sheep station in Australia and come to Canada to set up a sheep farm on the Millstream Road land. John realized that his father's 300 acres of rock and trees were not suitable for raising sheep.

Telephone poles cut and sold by John at 50 cents a pole brought in some money, as did John's job with the B. C. Electric. He also joined the Canadian Scottish reserve unit for extra income, and that was the beginning of the illustrious military career of Major General John Meredith Rockingham.

Walter Rockingham sold the Millstsream Road property after his wife Ethel died in 1941. He moved to Halifax where he began a new career in his sixties as a financial manager in a chartered accounting firm, then retired to the west coast again at the age of 82. Walter and Ethel are buried in Hatley Park Cemetery, as are his son and daughter-in-law, John and Mary Carlyle (Hammond) Rockingham.

AFTER WORLD WAR II

Land for a community hall was bought with funds raised by the Women's Auxiliary of the Langford Community Association. Langford's first fire truck was garaged in the basement of the hall, which was also known as the Buffalo Hall. When the larger fire hall was built on Goldstream Avenue the building was moved to the Luxton Fair Grounds and became Middleton Hall.

The Jacobsen family bought 10 acres of land near the old school in 1947 when a dirt trail became Jacklin Road.

The Knotty Pine Restaurant deserves a mention as Langford's most sophisticated dining place in the 1950s and 60s. The coffee shop was casual, but owner and chef Ernest von Hempel expected suitably formal attire for his memorable meals in the dining room.

The Knotty Pine Restaurant deserves a mention as Langford's most sophisticated dining place in the 1950s and 60s.

The multi-use St. Anthony's medical centre began as a one-story clinic and pharmacy on land that had once been Hayward's chicken farm and a piggery.
(Juan de Fuca News photo.)

The Island Highway (Goldstream Avenue) west of the village was little more than a country road on the way up-island even in the 1930s. Jack Taylor's Garage was a convenient stop for motorists heading for the arduous trip up the Malahat – a chance to check gas, tires, and extra water before the big hill. It was also memorable for its pool table. Jack Taylor built the Langford Speedway between his garage and Langford School in 1936. (BC Archives E-00500)

The Forest Ranger station at the south east corner of the Goldstream/Millstream intersection was a 1937 addition to the Langford streetscape. The distinctive gambrel-roofed administrative headquarters, dormitories and workshops occupied the site of the present Veterans Memorial Park, created in 2001 after the buildings were demolished. When the Forest Service left in 1969 the buildings were used by the Goldstream Museum, the Canadiana Costume Museum and the Westshore Chamber of Commerce. (M. Duffus Photo)

The Nite Owl, better known as the trolley diner, was on or near the present Litz Centre at the corner of Spencer Road and Goldstream Avenue, conveniently near the Langford Speedway. It was advertised in a Speedway program in the early 50's as "Vancouver Island's only streetcar diner, Opposite Langford Community Hall." Note the juke boxes on the counter. (BC Archives D-07564, D-07565)

Jacklin Road, now a major connector between Goldstream and Sooke Road, didn't exist when Allan LeQuesne and his friends Kenny and John Pringle raced their soapbox carts down the hill in what was then an extension of Station Road curving south toward Glen Lake. The picture was taken in the 1940s. (LeQuesne photo)

Since the restaurant closed the building's occupants have included a field office for the Provincial Ministry of Social Development (social welfare) and a dental office.

The first rectory of tiny St. Richard's Mission Church, which served the Catholic parishioners from 1948 until Our Lady of the Rosary Church was completed, was originally the home of Gertrude (Scafe) Aikman and her husband. The hall was a former army hut. (Fund raising efforts by Father Kennedy were ingenious but not altogether successful. They included purchase of a surplus war plane to dismantle and sell parts for scrap. Sales were not brisk, and neighbours were not pleased at the hill of scrap next door. Someone took it away for a price.

8

HAPPY VALLEY

(LANGFORD SECTION)

The story is that Happy Valley got is name from its first settlers, free black families who came to Victoria at the invitation of Governor James Douglas in 1858, happy to be safe from the troubles to the south. Freedom in a British colony was an attractive alternative to the anti-Negro sentiments of Californians of the time. The black settlers moved on, but the small valley that gives the larger area its name is still peaceful secluded farmland, hidden from the road by a fringe of trees.

Joseph Rhode stands at the back in shirtsleeves in this group of early Happy Valley pioneers. Charles Lorenzo Letoria is seated left. (Latoria Road was misnamed at some point in Happy Valley's history). The women and children are not identified.
(Metchosin School Museum)

Four years after the road improvement was completed Joseph Rhode bought 1,200 acres of land on both sides of Happy Valley Road...

The original trail through Happy Valley from Langford to Metchosin was widened to a wagon road in 1878. Tenders submitted to the Lands and Works Commissioner were opened on August 10 with four bids ranging from Samuel Morrow's $1,298 to William Gardner's $4,900, with Anderson and Irwin's estimates at $1,945 and Duncan McDonald at $1,970. The trail was upgraded to a road by 1880.

Four years after the road improvement was completed Joseph Rhode bought 1,200 acres of land on both sides of Happy Valley Road, including Glen Lake and extending south from Dicker Road to the part of Station Road that later became Jacklin Road.

Joseph Rhode came to Canada from Germany as a young man. He first lived over his bake shop on Store Street in Victoria, then moved to Happy Valley in 1884 with his second wife, Angelina Piaggio, and his children, Joseph, Frank and Pauline. Their son Albert was born in the house which stood across from the old store near the present Hazelwood Street. Sheep and cattle pastured on the farm where bear, cougar and wolves were a constant danger. The house was a hospitable stopping place for horse-and-buggy travellers on their way to Metchosin and Sooke.

Joseph continued farming until his death in 1907, when the farm was sold to Arthur Luxton, a law partner of Charles Pooley. The Rhode sons later returned to the valley, buying back some of the land once owned by their father. Frank and Albert built houses on the east side of the road around 1911, and brought up their families there. (Notes on the Rhode family are from Joseph's granddaughter, Violet Rainey, in conversation and from her family story in the Metchosin history *Footprints*.)

Records of other early settlers are scarce, but the population was large enough by 1896 for Happy Valley to have its own post office. Walter Poole was postmaster from the day it opened on August 1 until he resigned in June 1900. Other postmasters were James G. Walker, W. W. Winter, Charles Francis and Stuart Hutchison. Rural mail delivery replaced many of the local post offices in 1922.

Plans for subdividing part of the Luxton property were drawn up in 1911 when a railway to Sooke and Cowichan was expected to pass through the area and greatly increase the value of the land. Other owners of large properties included W. J. McArthur and R. Bray of Bray's Cartage Company whose land ran alongside the E. & N. railway tracks between Langford Lake and Glen Lake. Albert Hull bought property along Langford Lake from Mr. Bray and gave his name to the controversial potato fields – fertilizer from the agricultural activities drained into the lake with unfortunate results.

Arthur Philip Luxton is remembered because of the land he bought from Joseph Rhode, although it is unlikely he ever lived there. He came to Canada from England in 1888 as a 25-year-old solicitor, and was admitted to the British Columbia bar in 1890. He married Mary Clendenning Martin, daughter of an Ontario lawyer, in 1899, and was made King's Counsel in 1905. Like his law partner Charles Pooley, Q.C., he was a member of the Union Club. His biography lists his interests as golf, cricket and hunting, and notes he was "a member and director of several financial commercial and industrial enterprises of British Columbia." (Howay and Scholefield History of British Columbia, Biographies, Vol. IV, 1914)

(photo courtesy Bonnie Josephson)

Luxton had its own post office at the corner of Happy Valley Road and Sooke Road where Mrs. Jessie Luff was postmistress from opening day, August 1, 1911, to May 1914. George Heaslip, Mrs. Frances Heaslip, Walter Dallimore and Major Arthur C. Sutton, DSO, filled the position until the post office closed in 1922. The building later housed The Stump Coffee Shop.

(Dorothy Blenkinsop photo)

The Malvern Coffee Bar at the side of the house known as Loma Linda on Happy Valley Road was a popular meeting place for a few years. The owners, the Barker family, had a sawmill behind the house. A railway spur ran to the mill from the Canadian National tracks in the 1930s. The carefully restored house recently received a heritage award.
(Bonnie Josephson collection)

Land sales for the first subdivisions were slow until after World War I when the Soldiers' Settlement Act, a Canadian Government project, offered loans to veterans to buy farm land. Unfortunately the local Soldiers' Settlement Board purchased several lots along Happy Valley Road without considering a major problem: floods. By 1928 district engineer E. G. Marriott and his assistant D.K. Penfold prepared a list of families who had purchased or were renting from the SSB. They found residents were "greatly inconvenienced" by water covering much of the land right up to the buildings in the rainy seasons. Other property owners from Glen Lake to Dewdney Flats had problems as bad as, or worse than, the Settlement Board properties. Overflow from Bilston Creek, inadequate road culverts, water backing up along the railway and other widespread drainage problems contributed to the "inconvenience."

No one ever made a fortune farming in Happy Valley, what with floods and global problems like the 1930s depression which brought diminishing markets for produce. Families grew vegetables for their own use and for sharing with neighbours who might need help. Most families kept hens and cows so no one went hungry. Men worked at whatever outside jobs were available on the railway, with logging crews, construction or saw milling.

School time memories during World War I were recalled by three of the former Happy Valley School pupils, Grace (Henry) Robertson, Mabel (Henry) Muir and Irene (Carter) Pearson:

Someone brought a team of horses, far right, and nearly everyone, including a dog, turned up for the momentous flag raising at Happy Valley School shortly after it was built in 1911. Five Letoria children and Eddie Ross are standing in front of the pole. Behind them are Mr. and Mrs. Charles Letoria and Mr. and Mrs. Stockand. Helpers standing at right include Mr. Blatchford, Mr. McDougal, Gordon Cosh, David Henry, Mr. Hankin and Bill Woodruff. Classes began in January, 1912. Miss Lucy E. Gibson was the first teacher. Other teachers were Miss Quackenbush from Ontario, Miss Florence Down from England, Miss Everett from Ontario, and Mr. Sivertz, Mrs. McKenzie and Miss Bird, all from Victoria.
(Metchosin School Museum Society)

Miss Florence Down's pupils were photographed in 1913, when there were more than 30 children in the six grades that she taught throughout World War I. Note the high button boots on the feet dangling from the high bench in the front row. Left to right are John Stockand, Chris Rhode, Frank Letoria, Dorothy McKay, Inza Barker, Waverley Bruce, Trixie Smith, Gladys Dallimore, Claude Holman, Eddie Ross and Bruce Gray. Behind them, middle row, are Grace Henry, Hazel Barker, Amy Luff, Mabel Gould, Mabel Henry, Eileen Porter, Irene Carter, Waneta Letoria, Thelma Smith and Miss Down. Back row left to right are Jack Smith, Harold Badger, Charles Letoria, Frank Badger, Charlie Porter and Ross Gray.
(Metchosin School Museum)

"During Miss Down's tenure the school population increased when several families arrived from Ontario. They had been told that fifty cent pieces could be picked up on the streets of Victoria. There were two families named Barker. One started a mill along the railway tracks near Bilston Creek. The other Barker family had children at the school, Hazel, Ina and Lenore. Ross and Bruce Gray and Mabel Gould and Emerson Showers also came to school. Miss Everett taught during the war years and we can remember her marching the whole school down to an army camp somewhere near Glen Lake and off Station Road. We had Victory Gardens in the school grounds where we grew vegetables as our war effort. We remember our

The little schoolhouse in 1918-19, Edna T. Bird, teacher, and Irene (Carter) Pearson, janitress, in the doorway. The present Happy Valley Elementary School is on the same site.
(Metchosin School Museum)

teacher, Henry Sivertz, coming to say goodbye to our family before leaving for overseas. He was killed in action.

"Most of the children took their lunches to school in lard pails. In good weather we ate outside, often near a large old stump in the back of the schoolyard. Bilston Creek overflowed one year crossing the road near our home. We waited for our Dad to come for us, but when he didn't arrive we walked through the water and found that the wagon tongue had fallen and made quite a gash on father's head."

THE BRITISH VETERANS – 1920S

Many more families came during and after World War I. When Mr. and Mrs. Dick Oliver were married in 1920 the list of neighbours who contributed towards a gift for the popular couple reads like a Who's Who of Happy Valley: Browns, Blatchfords, Bakers, Brices Batchelors, Carter, Cole, Dalimore, Farger, Field, Gawley, Hutson, Hankin, Hutchinson, Jepson, Johnson, Kennedy, Lund, McLeod, McEway, Mills, Masters, Narraway, Pearson, Richards, Rhode, Stockand, Taylor, Temple, Winter, and Major and Mrs. Jones. The list in the back of the clock presented to them as a wedding gift was found many years later by their son, John Oliver, who still lives on part of the old farm.

Mr. and Mrs. F.W. Baker, who had moved away in 1923, returned to Happy Valley for a short visit which they described as "nine perfectly happy days of companionship with this group of sincere friends,

The list in the back of the clock presented to them as a wedding gift was found many years later by their son, John Oliver, who still lives on part of the old farm.

who vied with each other in hospitality and kindness." The family had lived on Happy Valley Road for four years on a farm near Neild Road (which used to be called Baxter Road). Many of the their friends are described in their holiday journal called *The Bakers' Round,* printed in 1932. They give a glimpse of the life and struggles of the British immigrants who came to Happy Valley during and just after World War I.

Mr. and Mrs. Baker and their young daughters stayed with Mr. and Mrs. Harry Baxter, in the large house Harry Baxter built himself. The journal notes that Harry "had tired of business life in London, sold his home in Beckenham and brought his wife and son and daughter to Happy Valley shortly after World War I. Having bought *Deerfoot* by paying too much for it as was the usual procedure they took to their new life in a remarkable way. He rigged up all sorts of gadgets, including the harnessing of miniature rapids and falls, ran the whole gamut of attempting to farm a somewhat rocky and shallow soil, kept all sorts of animals from rabbits, pigs and sheep to cows, feathered fowl, ducks and geese. Found they did nothing towards keeping him and abandoned the struggle without at any time losing his sense of humour." Mr. Baxter apparently found that "his expert knowledge of furs acquired in their business at home was more profitable than farming could ever be, but they stayed on the farm with no desire to leave. Their daughter Gladys married and moved to the Prairies, while their son Arthur stayed and went into the lumber business."

Mr. Baker described his friend Stuart Hutchinson as "an old soldier who served his country in Egypt, where he took part in the historic incident at Fashoda between French and British forces.[1] Then through the South African campaign after which he took his discharge and settled in Canada. The outbreak of the Great War saw him joining up with the Canadians. After the Armistice and a brief spell as physical instructor at a school he took the ill advised step of buying a farm under the newly formed Soldiers' Settlement Board, used his small capital in paying down the ten per cent required and is now anchored to an unproductive piece of land unable to raise

---

1   This explains the naming of Fashoda Place off Happy Valley Road. The incident involved French and British expeditions in a rush to claim land for their countries in Africa. Both reached Fashoda, a village on the Upper Nile in the Sudan, at about the same 1898. Common sense prevailed in London and Paris before the two countries went to war over an Egyptian village. Stuart Hutchinson must have served with the larger British force under Lord Kitchener. (From The Open Door Web Site)

enough to keep his family of four, let alone pay any more towards the figure at which his 'farm' was valued. Hiring himself with his horses, while he could keep them, for ploughing; working in the woods, doing odd jobs on the roads and wherever he could get them. His plucky wife has helped out by district visiting and nursing."

Fred and Rosie Batchelor were the nearest neighbours during the Baker family's four years in Happy Valley, and "ever present helps in times of trouble and need. Did we need advice as to jam making or other domestic mysteries Rosie was cheerfully available. Was a carpentry or other job rather too heavy for us or beyond our amateurish skill, Fred instantly responded to our S.O.S. Early on Good Friday a batch of hot cross buns in the making of which he excelled invariably came before we were up. Rosie's specialty was making butter and Devonshire cream at which she was an expert. Good neighbours and two of the best."

Fred was also a South African veteran who joined the Hemel Hemptead volunteers and spent a time with the South African Constabulary before emigrating to Canada. He too lost no time in joining up at the outbreak of World War I with the 16th Canadian Scottish. He met his wife in England and brought her to Canada to share the ups and downs on another Soldiers' Settlement Board Farm called *Mutley* after the district in Plymouth were Rosie's sister lived.

During his military service Fred collected dozens of shrapnel splinters which caused him pain and handicapped him badly in his work, but he was denied a disability pension because the Pensions Board doctors diagnosed his back trouble as lumbago. In spite of spells of illness the Batchelors worked hard to keep up the payments on their farm. They were helped by a nephew from England, Walter Whybrow, who won a sweepstake which he used to pay off the final installment due on the farm

The Bakers also write about Dick and Marjorie Oliver and their three children who lived at *Quality Farm*. "Another old soldier who had served in the Boer War, hailing from Yorkshire, Dick had settled here with his brother and gone in for chickens, cows and an occasional pig to drink up the skim and bring home the bacon." He remembered the countless times Dick "helped out with chicken problems, kept down a plague of rats with the help of his terrier Biddy; gave freely of his time in cultivating our potato patch, using

"Did we need advice as to jam making or other domestic mysteries Rosie was cheerfully available."

"Another old soldier who had served in the Boer War…"

his own horse and machine; cooking and bringing over special tidbits such as spare ribs, his speciality as chef. Then again his unerring shotgun was mainly instrumental in keeping down coons and hawks, two great causes of premature mortality among the chickens."

Mr. and Mrs. Alfred Hankin, who had looked after Rosemary Baker's Shetland pony in their orchard, also provided hospitality. "Mr. Hankin came to Canada with his father, a retired bank manager from the Old Country, spent some years farming on the prairies and then moved on to British Columbia where his father died at a ripe old age. Alfred devotes a great deal of his time and energies in public work [and was] chairman of trustees for the local school. In addition Alfred Hankin was the agent for a political party and very much to the fore at election times." Mrs. Hankin, the former Peggy Dyer, was a sister of one of the earlier teachers at Happy Valley School.

During their stay the Bakers recaptured some of the atmosphere of bygone days. Mr. Baxter says he had the time of his life splitting wood one morning and was gratified to learn that "the morning's work had resulted in enough stove-wood split and stacked to last a week. The girls picked loads of blackberries from a practically inexhaustible supply, as it didn't matter how many berries failed to reach the pails."

They attended a service at the Trinity Mission Church "meeting friends in the place we had met so regularly in the days when old Mr. Winter was the rector. Then Patty Hutchinson drove us to Glen Lake, one of nature's beauty spots where the younger fry – Esther, Catherine, Elsie and George Hutchinson with our pair – indulged in swimming until dusk. Our only full Sunday in the Valley was completely rounded off by a supper party at the Baxters."

They still had time to spend with Sid and Sarah Brice, whose well-stocked library had always been at the Baker's disposal, and Mr. and Mrs. Alfred Weeks "at their tidy little house and chicken ranch." Then they saw Mrs. Stockand, "the only pukka Canadian born of all the Valley people, I believe We were sorry that Mr. Stockand had passed on a few years previously." They paid a call on Mrs. Rhode while Mr. Rhode was unfortunately away at work, and Mr. and Mrs. Dan Ruddle were kind hosts another day. "Mr. Ruddle is brother to Mrs. Winter ... the Ruddles had left the Old Country for the great open spaces of Canada but had not found it all they expected.

Happy Valley families gathered for the sod turning of Trinity Mission Church in 1912. Identified in the back row are Mr. Cosh, Ivy Cosh, Miss Quackenbush (teacher), Joyce Ridley, Mrs. D. Henry, Mr. M. Blatchford, Bishop Brewing (?), Rev. W. W. Winter, Rev. T. W. Gladstone, Mrs. Flesch and Delwin(?) and Gordon Cosh. The Ladies are Mrs. Dan Ruddle, Mrs. Winter, Miss Marjorie Winter, Mrs. Luff, with Grace Henry, Esther Neild and Amy Luff in behind. The children in the front row are Aletha Shields Gladys Flesh, Irene Carter, Mabel Henry, Margherita Leteria, Eileen Porter, Louisa Letoria, Helen Cosh, Clarence and Eugene Flesh and Charles Porter. (Metchosin School Museum)

Another connection with the Winters with whom we spent a pleasant afternoon was the daughter of Mr. and Mrs. Winters, now Mrs. Lee Field, and children who lived on a big farm with her husband and his brother Chester Field. The farm is big enough to carry two establishments – Mrs. Field senior with Chester and a companion in one house and Lee's family in the other."

Lastly, they had time to see Mrs. and Mrs. Bob Brown and the Dallimores. "Mr. Dallimore came from Frome, Somersetshire. He provided a regular freight service driving his lorry into Victoria and bringing back orders for friends at a very modest charge. Mrs. Dallimore ran a stall in the [city] market twice a week and between them they got along. Mr. Dallimore led a useful generous life in service to his fellows as warden and general helper at the church, always

Rev. W. W. Winter instigated the formation of Trinity Mission Church which was connected with the Episcopalian Church of Our Lord in Victoria. It stood near Winter Road and served the small population of Happy Valley until 1939. It was demolished in the 1940s.
(Metchosin School Museum)

willing to drive parties of neighbours or Sunday School children to picnics."

On the last night of their holiday in Happy Valley the Bakers wrote "It was fitting that the last night of our stay should be celebrated at a big affair at Luxton Hall where such community gatherings were held, and we were glad to meet nearly everybody we had known in the district. Everyone helps at these functions and most enjoyable concerts, dances, whist drives and suchlike take place at frequent intervals. The supper provided by all bringing something was the most pleasant part of the affair. But the men would get and keep together, probably because this was their only chance to exchange views on subjects more congenial to the masculine mind.

Hence it was a common sight to see the sexes well separated and perfectly contented to be so. We have memories of a series of entertainments we were largely instrumental in running, and at which we tried to induce the husbands and wives to sit together – with indifferent success – it just wasn't done."

The journal was printed in Shanghai where Mr. Baker was editor of the Shanghai Times.

"...we tried to induce the husbands and wives to sit together – with indifferent success – it just wasn't done."

HAPPY VALLEY HALL

The old Happy Valley community hall was built at the beginning of World War I, thanks to the energetic Mrs. Mary Cooper. She had organized dances for young people in the one-room Happy Valley School, as well as the weekly dances to raise money for the Red Cross when war broke out in 1914. In a burst of Puritanism some school authorities deemed the dances inappropriate events for school premises and put a stop to the frivolity.

Mrs. Cooper (the same Mary Porter who had lived on Captain Langford's farm as a child) then determined that the community should build a hall of its own. She persuaded a local landowner, Francis Eugene Reid, to allow construction of a hall on his property. A committee was formed, lumber was bought from Barker's mill up the road, and volunteers completed the two-storey building in less than a year for a few hundred dollars. John Oliver remembers the dance floor made of two-inch fir was carefully taken apart by a Mr. Heath and relaid in the lower hall after the upper storey was removed.

Happy Valley Hall had a name change in 1925 to Luxton Hall when the area at the north end of Happy Valley became known as Luxton. Glen Lake corner at the junction of Happy Valley Road and Sooke Road was then known as Luxton Corners. The hall was run by elected hall committees until the late 1960s when the Metchosin Farmer's Institute took over management and hired a caretaker who lived on site.

The hall has been used for many community activities over the years: basketball games, dances, political meetings, wedding parties and club meetings. Minutes of committee meetings show that the young girls' Busy Bees group paid for hall rental with firewood in 1925. Newspaper clippings report an even wider variety of events

In a burst of Puritanism some school authorities deemed the dances inappropriate events for school premises and put a stop to the frivolity.

...the young girls' Busy Bees group paid for hall rental with firewood in 1925.

and their sponsors at the hall in the 1940s: a talk on preventive dentistry for Happy Valley Luxton Association; flower shows with decorated tables, home cooking, candy and a superfluity stall; a dance under the auspices of the Glen Lake Tennis and Badminton Club; a card party; a tulip tea by the Junior Red Cross of Happy Valley School; a sermon with lantern slides and a school Christmas concert. During World War II women of the area organized many social events for young servicemen and women.

THE LUXTON FALL FAIR

Agricultural fairs have been a part of western communities history for nearly a century. The first were sponsored by the Metchosin Farmers' Institute when it included farmers throughout the area from Parson's Bridge to Sooke. Early gatherings at harvest time were more like workshops or seminars with experts on hand to discuss livestock and crop programs. The first fairs moved around the districts from Metchosin to Colwood until the present site was purchased in 1928. Mr. Reid, an absentee landowner, agreed to subdivide part of his land behind the community hall for the Metchosin Farmers' Institute. They bought 1.8 acres for $400, according to a Land Registry document signed by local lawyer and institute member J. Stuart Yates. Over the years more land has been added to bring the total area to approximately 15 acres to accommodate the popular annual fair. Fancy poultry, rabbits, even llamas, have almost entirely replaced sheep and cattle in the livestock buildings, but home baking, canned fruit, jams and jellies, are still entered for judging. Entries have come from many Langford families over the years.

More recently the display of heritage farm equipment collected and restored to working order by members of the Metchosin Farmers Institute has been a major attraction each year. Heritage displays also include collections of photographs and newspapers from pioneer days.

The first fairs moved around the districts from Metchosin to Colwood until the present site was purchased in 1928.

THE OLDEST FARM

Morwena Farm had for many years one of the most photographed barns between Victoria and Sooke. The land was first farmed by Henry Cogan, an Englishman who came to Victoria in the 1860s. He sold the farm to a member of the Douglas family who sold it to Edgar Dewdney, who figures prominently in British Columbia history: first as a member of Colonel Moody's staff in the Royal Engineers who surveyed the townsite of New Westminster; as a member of the provincial legislature, and representative for Yale in the federal government, and as the fifth lieutenant governor of British Columbia in the 1890s. He lived at the Sooke Road farm for a short time in 1906, long enough to leave his name to the low-lying property on both sides of the Sooke Road. Best known of more recent owners was Herm Williams, whose dairy and cattle farm supplied milk to many Victoria outlets including the Northwestern Creamery. More recently the land was farmed by industrious Chinese for many years. The fields near the highway were part of the ancient flood plain and yielded fine crops, but the narrow section of Sooke road was often under several feet of water after heavy rains.

The old farmhouse at Dewdney Flats at Langford's southern boundary was the home of 19th century pioneers Henry Cogan and his wife, Mary Charlotte Robson. The Sooke Road farm later belonged to British Columbia's Lieutenant Governor Edgar Dewdney, and more recently to Herm Williams who is remembered for his flourishing Morwena Dairy. (Victoria City Archives 98404-41-4404)

The picturesque old timbered barn on the Dewdney Flats was a photogenic landmark at the south west boundary of Langford for many years. It was slowly taken apart by people salvaging seasoned fir planks until it was dangerously near collapse, and finally fell in a heap A building at the rear was used as a dormitory for the Chinese farmers, according to notes from Ken Cameron. (Bonnie Josephson photo)

GETTING TO THE CITY

In the 1920s and 30s, before every family had an automobile, a day in town to shop at the Hudson's Bay Company or the David Spencer department stores was a bit of an expedition. Horse and wagon gave way to motorized vehicles, starting with the famous jitney that picked up passengers from Metchosin to View Royal.

The Veteran Stages company, started by Stan Turner, eventually became a major transportation company for the western communities under the ownership of Arthur Wale. The busses went to the 700 block Yates Street for 35 cents, or 50 cents return. Children rode

Jitney service was the first motorized public bus service in the western communities. This photo was taken at the corner of Wharf and Government streets before the service station with a tower was built at the end of the causeway. A sign on the side advertises Campbell's drug store.
(BC Archives E-04066)

The Veteran Stages busses were preceded by Arthur Wale's smaller vehicles, a Ford, a Studebaker and a McLaughlin, described as "all top-notch vehicles suited to bussing service in their time." As the business expanded more drivers were hired. One of the new drivers, Robert Bugslag, remarked on a trip to Langford "How can you live out here with all that noise from the frogs?"
(Francis Wale Photo)

free. Later the terminus was moved to Herald and Douglas streets across from the Hudson's Bay store.

The Canadian National Railway also provided passenger service for 30 on a gasoline-powered car. The 'train' was equipped with a small baggage and mail compartment and operated by one man who served as engineer, conductor and trainman. The CNR line was primarily used by logging companies at Cowichan

Timetables in Clarke's Handy Guide for 1924 and 1926 in Ben Swindell's collection show the C.N.R Motor Car Service made two trips 'daily except Sunday' from its Point Ellice Station, stopping at Parson's Bridge, Glen Lake and Happy Valley on its way to and from Cowichan. The E.&N. Railway also stopped at Langford Station (called Colwood until later in the 1920s) and Goldstream.

Gas-powered car on CN tracks picked up passengers from Happy Valley to View Royal for a few years in the 1920s.
(Elwood White photo)

9

GOLDSTREAM FAMILIES

Some permanent residents were living in Goldstream by the 1890s and early 1900s. A few farmers took advantage of the fertile soil around the lakes which became Victoria's watershed, but other residents worked at the water works, the powerhouse or the railway.

A British Columbia directory for 1899 gives a population figure of about 50. It lists eight farmers, including E. A. Carlow and George Woodruff; William Ralph, foreman at water works; E. Sketch, teamster; J. G. Thomson, railway section man and W. Thomson, track inspector; A. Taylor, merchant and farmer, and Robert Wilson, assistant electric engineer. By 1900 B. McClure was caretaker at the power plant and Richard McClure was a foreman at the Esquimalt waterworks along with George Wood. Newcomers by 1904 included Hugh McKnight, farmer; William Payne, farmer and carpenter and, later, a member of the school board; Adam Ross, waterworks foreman; William Watts, trackman, and several miners.

By 1910 the famous resort hotel was still attracting visitors under new owners, Mr. and Mrs. William Miller. Alexander Gilmore, an early owner of the first humble Goldstream House on the old wagon road, died in 1910 at the age of 86. His son-in-law and daughter, James and Mary (Molly) Phair, sold their popular 'new' hotel and surrounding land in 1909 and disappeared from Langford history. James died in Vancouver in 1942 at the age of 89, predeceased by Molly ten years earlier at 74.

Charles Edward Pooley, Q.C., a keen huntsman pictured here with a groundsman or gamekeeper, bought James Phair's Goldstream Hotel and surrounding property in 1909. "He was a man of magnificent physique, six feet two inches in height with a powerful frame, and he commanded attention in any gathering," his biographers said. Pooley was a well-known Victoria lawyer and member of the B.C. Legislature for 22 years, including seven years as Speaker of the House. (BC Archives F-02517)

Charles Pooley, a well-known lawyer and politician, bought the entire 1100 acre property from James Phair. He was born in Huntingdonshire, England in 1845, and came to Canada in 1862. After a short unsuccessful period of prospecting during the Cariboo gold rush he began studying law. From 1867 to 1879 he traveled with Judge Matthew Baillie Begbie as registrar of the Supreme Court of British Columbia which had become a province of Canada in 1871. He was called to the bar in 1877 and became a partner of A. E. Davie, Q.C. He was a director of many companies, including the Esquimalt Water Works.

Pooley sold the hotel and 33 acres to William Miller and his wife, May (Mary) Greening Miller, for $15,000 in 1910, but kept the Phair house and the rest of the property. When he died in 1912 the valuable property passed to his son and law partner. Alex Turner and his wife Amy bought the remaining acres and the large Phair home from the Pooley estate in 1939.

The Millers

Mr. and Mrs. William Miller of Vancouver ran the Goldstream Hotel as owner managers until Mr. Miller was killed in an automobile accident on the Malahat in 1915. Mrs. Miller continued as owner of the business with her niece, Daisy Cairns, as manager until the building was destroyed by fire in 1923.

May (Mary) Greening was born in St. John's, Newfoundland, in 1877 and came to Vancouver with her family in 1906 after living in Boston for 15 years. She married her second husband, Asa Smith, a "prominent local horse breeder," in 1929. She was referred to as May Greening Miller-Smith on official documents, but Ma Miller to her customers in later years. Mrs. Miller also owned the Colwood Hotel which she operated for six years after the Goldstream fire, but retained ownership of the Goldstream property. She sold the Colwood Hotel property for $15,000 to George T. Quincy and used the money to rebuild the Goldstream Inn as a beer parlour in 1930.

Her favourable financial situation was assessed by an inspector from the Liquor Control Board in 1930 when she applied for a liquor licence : "… [the Millers] purchased the Goldstream Hotel property … in 1910 for $15,000, paying down $2500. She later became the owner & conducted the hotel until being burnt out at Goldstream

Ma Miller: Mary 'Ma' Miller Smith was described by an inspector from the Liquor Control Board as "beyond middle age and married, a resident of this district for years, also at Colwood." He approved of the lady who was "reputed of steady habit, & fair general reputation. What success she is meeting with in present location not determined, stand being only a fair one for this line. Future prospects fair." His assessment of business prospects was unduly pessimistic: the business has since prospered without interruption for more than 70 years. (Photo Courtesy Cindy Piga, Goldstream Inn)

January 30, 1923. Carried insurance on building of $10,000 & $4,000 on contents, including stock of cigarettes, cigars etc., and also $1,000 on furniture and effects … Amount of loss never determined but it is believed that she was fully covered." She was reported as "prompt in payments in trade quarters and quoted in good credit standing."

Her application for a liquor licence for the new establishment, a beer parlour, brought objections from unlikely sources. The Loggers Association of BC, a Washington State logging company, the City of Victoria and the Prohibition League of Victoria all wrote letters to the Liquor Control Board opposing Mrs. Miller's proposal to sell beer.

The Loggers Association and the logging company warned that a beer parlour at Goldstream "would be a menace to the well fare of the men." The chairman of the Loggers Association wrote that "it would be impossible to prevent men from making a daily visit to a beer parlor when only a short distance away from camp, should they so desire, with the result, that a percentage of men would be on the job at the commencement of a days' work with anything but alert minds, to avoid the many hazards met with in our Industry." The objection, he insisted, was in the interests of accident prevention, not at all with a view of "preventing men from obtaining refreshments at a proper time or place." The logging company feared that their efforts to reduce accidents would be undermined by "the location of a beer parlor in this vicinity … [which] will be a stimulant to their [accidents'] increase."

F.M. Preston, Victoria's city engineer and water commissioner, was of the opinion that "the granting of this license would not be in the public interest" and would make enforcement of provincial health regulations in the watershed harder." A dismissive hand-written comment in the margin of the water commissioner's letter reads:[1] "This is a frivolous protest as the intake and drainage area of Victoria water supply is a long way off and many hundreds of feet higher than the ground in question." Then the Prohibition League worried that

"it would be impossible to prevent men from making a daily visit to a beer parlor when only a short distance away from camp, should they so desire…"

Then the Prohibition League worried that the neighbourhood "should be kept free from the temptation which a beer parlor would doubtless provide."

1   These were typical objections in the post-prohibition days when liquor was available only at government stores and in drinking establishments which were required to have two entrances, one for men and a separate section for ladies and escorts. Some sections of Greater Victoria elected to remain 'dry' while others like Esquimalt and Goldstream voted to allow carefully regulated sale of beer only. Wine and hard liquor were not permitted.

The Goldstream Inn in 2002, much as it appeared when it was rebuilt in 1930 on the site of the 1886 resort hotel. The barn where Asa Smith kept his Goldstream Stables race horses was on the north side behind the hotel. A few reminders of the earlier hotel's glory days remained until the 1950s: the bandstand was across Humpback Road on the site of the present café and grocery store. The 1890s Militia rifle range was behind the hotel on fields now covered with a modern subdivision up to the boundary of the Water District. (M. Duffus photo)

the neighbourhood "should be kept free from the temptation which a beer parlor would doubtless provide."

But 'Ma' submitted a petition of her own signed by all but one of the local residents in favour of her application. May Greening Miller-Smith received Beer Licence No. 1815 on December 16, 1930, for the year 1931. She continued as owner-manager of the Goldstream Inn until she retired 15 years later.

The vanished resort hotel, reborn as a beer parlour in 1931, is now a welcoming neighbourhood pub under present owners Tony and Cindy Piga. Long-time customers recall that the Ma Miller they knew was a colourful personality, a clever businesswoman and a generous and community minded person. She died in 1966 at the age of 90. As a tribute to the friendly lady who came to the district in 1910 the Goldstream Inn is affectionately known as Ma Miller's.

Cindy Piga tells the story of a patron who came into the pub to ask the new owners if she was still barred. She explained that during the celebrations on D-day when the European war ended in 1945 Ma Miller barred the enthusiastic young lady for dancing on tables. Now older and less athletic, Hilda Tucker is a welcome customer at the pub.

The new owners also suspect there is a non-malignant ghost in the pub. "No-one sees it, but strange things happen, especially during construction or a change to the building," Cindy says. "I was working upstairs in the office one day when something went right through a row of coat hangers in a cupboard, jingling and jangling. No one else was in the building, there was no draft or any explanation." It was unnerving, as was the appearance of paper work all over the floor when someone doing the cash returned after a brief absence. One of the waitresses heard whispering when she was going upstairs. As yet there has not been a sighting.

The Adam Ross house at Goldstream in 1903, and the Ross family and friends in front of Humpback Road House at Japan Gulch, 1915, above right. (Family photos)

Adam Ross Family

Adam Ross came to live near the Humpback Reservoir as caretaker in the early 1890s. He stayed until 1938, through the years of World War I when soldiers were brought in to guard the water works. He was born in Ayrshire, Scotland in 1861 and came to Canada in 1883. He first lived at Sooke, 20 miles west of Victoria, where another Ayrshire family, the Muirs, settled in the 1860s. Adam married Marion Muir in 1885. Sadly Marion died after the birth of their daughter, Violet Mabel, in 1888. After his wife's death Adam moved to the house at Humpback Reservoir with his son, Thomas Michael, and daughter. He and his second wife, Margaret Gemmell, had five daughters, Margaret, Leila, Jean, Daisy and Edith. Adam's wife, Margaret, died a year before he retired after 48 years as caretaker at Goldstream. He moved to Colwood where he died in 1950 at the age of 89.

William Payne Family

William Payne bought land at Goldstream in 1904. He emigrated from London in 1890 and first worked for the City of Victoria public works department. He brought his wife, Hanna, and their children to a large farm near Humpback Reservoir, first to a log cabin and barn on high ground above a swamp, between the Phair house and the

Members of the Payne family at their farm on Humpback Road in the early 1900s. (Victoria City Archives 98304-41)

hotel. The swamp had fertile soil for a large vegetable garden, but was too wet to plant until the end of June, a disadvantage when Saanich growers harvested and sold their crops much earlier. Produce had to be transported on the train which stopped at Goldstream Station at noon and at 5 p.m. on the return trip to Victoria. William and his sons built the big home above Humpback Road in 1913. He stayed in the house alone after Hanna died in 1930 until his own death in 1951. Their older children moved to Victoria but their youngest son Jack, the only child born at Goldstream, and his wife Anne lived there until Anne died. Jack moved to Sidney in 2000. The water board now owns the property.

The other sons, Bill, Carl and Petrel also found work on the pipeline extensions to Victoria and the Bamfield life-saving trail. Bill was a reservist with the army when soldiers guarded the watershed at Japan Gulch in World War I. In 1915 he married Adam Ross's daughter Margaret at the caretaker's home.

Goldstream school children, ca. 1920. Jack Payne is second from right, back row. The future Mrs. Payne is far right (Victoria City Archives 98304-41)

The Carlows, Dixons and Goodalls

Edwin Carlow bought land in the Goldstream area in 1897. His farm was in what became the Goldstream Watershed, rich fertile land with swamps and meadows surrounded by forests. His brother William returned from the Klondike to join him, filled with stories of the gold rush and the trail of '98. After Edwin Carlow left his farm it was occupied by the Dixon family, then the Goodall family. When the Humpback reservoir and dam were built the house was moved across the road.

Alex Turner family

Alex and Amy Turner bought the property at the west end of Langford Lake, known in earlier days as Phair's fields, from the Pooley estate in 1939. The property extended from the corner of Sooke Lake and Humpback Roads down to Langford Lake, and included the large Phair house.

Alex Turner left Aberdeen, Scotland, at 16. He came to Vancouver Island by way of the United States and the Fraser Valley where he worked on a horse stud farm. He and Amy had three children, Edith, Eileen and Alex, when they operated a cattle ranch in north Saanich across from the Sandown race track. Eileen remembers the cattle drive from Saanich to

The Phair house when the Turner family lived there in 1959, and when the Phair family lived there ca. 1905. In the earlier picture Florence, Mabel and Viola Phair sit on the steps with a Miss Grant and another friend. Eileen Turner Smith remembers the house as large, but so cold in the winter the family had to live in the kitchen. The house and barns were approached from Humpback Road along a driveway south east of the Goldstream Inn. (View Royal Archives, left, and Turner family photo, above)

Possibly the last cows in Langford live on remaining acres of Turner Meadows where Alex Turner raised calves for dairy farmers and, later, prize-winning Black Angus cattle. Eileen Turner Smith still lives on the road named for her mother Amy. She is still growing fruit and vegetables in a small valley below the house, and has been winning prizes at fall fairs since she was a child.
(M. Duffus photo)

Goldstream when she was a child. She and her sister walked behind the animals from the Saanich farm, across the airport, south to Prospect Lake Road, finally to Millstream Road and on to Goldstream. Their father followed in a car as the girls stood in driveways to stop the cattle from detouring all along the route. The drive took two days with an overnight rest on Prospect Lake Road.

William Linton family

Alice Linton Hayes recalled childhood years in a house on the old Government Road near the Pond Lake in the watershed. Legend has it that this building was the first stop for ox-drawn wagons on their way from Victoria to the settlement at Cowichan. Alice believes the house was built much later, around 1912 when her father first came as an employee of the water district in charge of checking and changing levels of the lakes that fed the reservoir. (See Appendix IV)

"The first thing I remember is that we all had to have typhoid shots. Anyone living that close to the water supply was not allowed any communicable disease," she said in a recent interview. She also remembered the freedom of playing at the pond and across the dam. "Mother was not worried about letting her children go off to play in the woods, or at least she didn't let on. Of course there was no one else around. It didn't occur to us that we might get lost. We just figured out which way we had come, so that was the way we would go back. Perhaps we had more sense of direction than children these days."

Photo of Linton house in May, 2001, shows the venerable apple tree blossoming in the garden where Mrs. Linton grew impressive crops of fruit and vegetables to last the winter in their isolated home. Mr. Linton was a water board employee who regulated water levels in the system, including Cabin Pond. The upper storey was added later as dormitory space for workmen and guards patrolling the watershed.
(M. Duffus photo)

When Alice attended Goldstream School in the early 1930s she and her brother and older sister boarded during the week with the McKnight family who lived near the Humpback reservoir. It was a long walk from the Linton home to Humpback Road and then along the road to the school a mile or so on the far side of the railway tracks.

"We walked back from the McKnights on Fridays and father met us at the power station. Mr. Phipps, a superintendent, had a sound-proof office to the right of the big main doors where they played cards or chequers until we arrived. The powerhouse was really, really noisy. Usually there was only one turbine going, but sometimes two were running if needed.

"Then we had another long walk up the hill to our house, carrying our clothes and books on packboards father made for us. It was much easier after father got a car and drove us home from the power-house." Mrs. Hayes also remembers the store at the Sooke Lake Road corner, when the highway went nearby. The store would have been in the middle of what is now the road.

The dam at Cabin Pond where the Linton children used to play.
(M. Duffus photo)

The Thomson family on a hand-propelled rail cart for a Sunday outing in the late 1890s when John Thomson, centre back, was foreman of the Langford to Malahat section of the E. & N. railway. Charles "Ted" Thomson, who succeeded his brother in 1899, and another brother, Hugh, are at the left of the picture with Jack's two sons, his wife Sarah (Atkins) Thomson and their daughter Muriel enjoying the ride. (Goldstream Museum, donated by Margaret Giles)

Goldstream Station, ca. 1898, with section foreman John Thomson standing at front of steam-puffing locomotive. Far right, water tank beside the station, and right, E. & N. train crossing Arbutus Canyon, 1898. (Photos copied from old family prints by Philip Judd for Mrs. Giles, donated to Goldstream Museum)

John G. Thomson

John Thomson, known as Jack, was one of 15 children born to Saanich pioneers William and Margaret Thomson of 'Bannockburn', Mount Newton Crossroad. He was born there in 1871 and moved to Langford at the age of 18. He worked on the E. & N. Railway from Langford to the Goldstream Station and on the Malahat section, eventually as section foreman. His brother Charles, known as Ted, continued as foreman after Jack left in 1899 with his brother Robert to join their brothers, Walter and Richard, in South Africa. The older brothers had a contract to build streetcar rail tracks in Johannesburg.

Jack's eldest daughter, Margaret Thomson Giles, remembered traveling 'up-Island' with her brother Robert during holidays. They especially enjoyed the observation car, the end car of the train where they spent most of the journey that left them quite "sooty" by the time they reached Courtenay.

Rupert Stevens Family

The Stevens strawberry farm was one of the last agricultural enterprises before residential development overtook the area where Sooke Lake Road climbs to Humpback Road. Godfrey Stevens has fond memories of growing up there before his musician father Rupert sold the farm and left for Hollywood. In a telephone conversation and e-mail notes he emphasized the strong feeling in Goldstream that it was quite distinct from Langford.

Other recollections include: his dugout canoe, patched with tin cola signs nailed over cracks to keep out water, which he once took down the ditch that connects Langford Lake to Goldstream River where it got jammed in the weeds in the middle of Turners' meadow; having to pit lamp the deer which ate the crops, and donating the meat to the Salvation Army; playing in the old copper mines on Skirt Mountain with his brother Aaron, and finding a bat deep in a horizontal shaft; taking it home to fly around the living room of the blue-roofed house standing among the blue-roofed farm buildings.

His father sold the farm to finance a move to Hollywood, hoping to further his song-writing career. Sixteen-year-old Godfrey was reluctant to leave. The Hollywood venture wasn't a success, but some of the words of Rupert Stevens's song, *The Blue Green Hills of Goldstream* (see box), stay in his son's mind: "Something like that – sounds better with music and the right sequence," Godfrey admits.

> ### Rupert Stevens' Lyrics
> *The blue green hills of Goldstream*
> *Once swarmed with gold-crazed men*
> *Whose lusty oaths still echo*
> *In each gulf and lonely glen.*
> *Shy deer still nibble at salal,*
> *The blue grouse wings its way*
> *On mountain pools where loons' wild cry*
> *Still marks the end of day ...*

The Goldstream Berry Paradise fruit stand around 1950, on the Island Highway near Sooke Lake Road.
(Stevens Family photo)

The Phillips Turkey Farm

Geraldine Phillips has written about her adventures running a large turkey farming operation on Irwin Road. In *High Heels to Gumboots* she tells about the decision to move to the country in 1955 and the growth of the business which supplied turkeys, delivered by Geri herself, to restaurants and hotels, including the Empress Hotel.

Residential subdivisions now cover the fields around the original hotel site as far as the watershed property and a seniors' mobile home park occupies the hillside along Sooke Lake Road. Farther along Humpback Road the forest remains and land in the shadow of Mount Wells is still sparsely populated. The Goldstream Park campsite includes shady trails by the river and a small part of the old Government Road.

An old panorama photo of Langford Lake, looking south from Goodmanson's property, on a bluff across the Old Island Highway at the foot of Skirt Mountain. (Ken Hincks collection)

10
LAKES AND PARKS

Langford Lake has attracted Victorians for hunting and picnics since the Esquimalt and Nanaimo Railway opened up the country around it in the 1880s. Glen Lake was unknown to all but local families until another railway encouraged landowners to subdivide property around the lake for summer cottages. Florence Lake, less than half a mile north of the Trans Canada Highway, is still unknown to most Victorians. It is almost entirely surrounded by private property and cut off from the southern parts of Langford by the Trans Canada highway.

The original 1912 house has been home to the Merriman family since 1948.

LANGFORD LAKE

One of the earliest recorded picnic expeditions to Langford Lake was recalled by Martha Douglas Harris, youngest daughter of James and Amelia Douglas. She remembered "...the magnificent picnics that Dr. and Mrs. Tolmie gave ... at Langford Lake. They had all their servants out and all manner of gorgeous things to eat, such as turkeys, chickens, ducks, geese, hams, pies, everything complete; such a wonderful day as we spent there. There must have been 200

Barnsley Lodge was built at Langford Lake about 1904 by John Barnsley, owner of a sporting goods store in Victoria, on 49 acres of secluded wilderness. It was "a large log cabin with a huge comforting fireplace, fine food and comfortable beds - a welcome sight for local and out-of-town sportsmen and friends, relaxing atmosphere for hundreds of hunters. There were huge blue and willow grouse, pheasants, quails, ducks, bear, bass and trout," Hazel Olson wrote in her memoirs.
(Victoria City Archives PR24, #38)

guests present, such a beautiful summer day." Martha also recalled the procession of carriages needed to transport guests and food from town several years before the E. & N. Railway was completed in 1886.[1] From Pioneer Women of Vancouver Island.

Victoria hunters rediscovered the country around Langford Lake and the surrounding mountains in the 1890s, long after it was known as an abundant source of game for First Nations families.

Hazel Olson described the lake area as she remembered it in the early 1900s when her father, William Scafe, hunted there and knew the various hunting lodges at the lake.

"A dense forest of alder, fir, willow and cedar formed a barrier between the railroad and Langford Lake, hiding it from the view of train travelers. Barnsley Lodge was a popular wilderness hideaway near the far end of the lake. The lake was an enchanting lure for fishermen and hunters around 1900 set in semi-wild jungle-like terrain … particularly the north and west sides. The old rough gravel road [then part of the Victoria-Cowichan highway] was unsuitable for picnickers who much preferred Goldstream where there were pleasant cleared areas and a few accessible trails, as well as the popular Goldstream Hotel."

Jacob Hassenfraz, a Swiss, built his hunting cabin, Deer Lodge, on his 10-acre property near Lake End Road on the north side of the Highway at the foot of Skirt Mountain. Herman Hasenfratz, left, and Ford and Peter Bugslag were photographed at the log cabin in 1908. The lodge was used by the family in winter and summer. Claude Bugslag says his father Peter's hunting weekends consisted of playing cards all Friday night, hunting all day Saturday and returning home Sunday. (Victoria City Archives PR252-6894)

---

1   Dr. William Fraser Tolmie was Chief Trader in charge of the Hudson's Bay Company's Fort Nisqually near Tacoma, Washington, until he retired to Victoria in 1859. He died in 1886 after serving several terms as a member of the B.C. Legislature. Martha Douglas was born in 1854.

Florence, Mabel and Viola Phair of the Goldstream Hotel, boating on the lake with friends in the early 1900s. They lived on the hill above the lake near Humpback Road. (View Royal Archives, attributed to Duncan McTavish)

Langford Lake Store, known as Pop Baynes store, with the auto court cabins behind the store.
(Roy Tennent photo)

The cabins can still be seen across the 'highway' behind the store at the Leigh Road corner. (M. Duffus photo)

Work stopped for a smoke and a drink at the Teddy Bear Cabin which was built as a hunting lodge by Arthur and Horace Mansell. The Matson House was built on the site of this log cabin at the corner of Leigh Road and the old Island Highway. (Victoria City Archives 98301-01, PR-4679)

Goldstream Road was still a trail when the Powers sisters, Elizabeth and Mary, bought the Barnsley Lodge with its 49 acres on both sides of the road and 400 feet of lakefront in 1911. Powers Lane is the only remaining link with one of the first hunting lodges in the area. The property along the lake from Barnsley's to Lake End Road was subdivided in 1907 but the sisters remained in the up-dated hunting lodge for many more years.

John Wenger, a jewelry store owner in Victoria, bought land near the present Wenger Terrace. According to notes from a manuscript prepared for the Capital Regional District his first small log cabin was across the road on the Skirt Mountain side of the property. The log chalet was built later at Wenger Bay.

Summer cottages soon outnumbered the hunting lodges. A first-hand account of Langford's cottage country between 1913 and 1935 survives, thanks to letters and photographs Roberta Basustow Jones donated to the Goldstream Museum in 1987.

Roberta's father, Charles Basustow, chose the site for the cabin on Leigh Road on the advice of Ben Thomas, who was believed to have built the first cottage at the eastern end of the lake.

Lumber was brought from the train station by hired wagon. Early cottagers often travelled from Victoria by train and walked to the lake from Langford Station. Soon nearly everyone had motor cars

The Mansells, like their cousin Roberta, were descendants on their mother's side of the pioneer Parker family of Metchosin and Rocky Point. Roberta Basustow Jones was the great- granddaughter of John Parker Sr. who came to Victoria in 1862, following his son John Junior, a Craigflower Farm employee from 1853. Her grandmother Emma Parker, a daughter of the senior John Parker and sister of John Junior, married James Ure, an officer of the ship that brought them to Victoria in 1862.

Roberta Basustow Jones sent these summer snapshots to the Goldstream Museum. Her mother Gertrude Basustow "in her customary long skirt, white blouse and 'hug-me-tight' in front of the recently completed house" at Langford Lake:; Charles Basustow with a string of bass caught at the lake – "There were no trout in those days, just bass, catfish and sunfish;" Roberta herself on July 1, 1917. (Goldstream Museum)

and the summer population increased. Baynes Auto Court, one of the first in BC, rented the cabins for shorter holiday visits.

Basustow Family

Roberta wrote of the families she remembered from her childhood. The Leigh family cottage was at the end of the road by the railway tracks. They had two children, Monica and Selwyn, who had an Indian dugout canoe. Others at the "head of the lake" were the Newberrys, the Misses Freeman (one a teacher at North Ward School), the Dalbys, the Pedens, the Lipseys and the Matson family at the corner of Leigh Road and the old highway.

One day she and Doris Matson, watching from the Matson's kitchen window, saw a motorist flick a cigarette into the bush across the road. A fire started immediately. "I leapt a fence, grabbed a sack soaking in a water tub and rushed across the road to try to beat out the fire. Others were close behind to help put the fire out quickly – everyone was desperate to keep the fire from spreading to the nearby auto court and gas station. There was no volunteer fire department in those days, and not too much help from forestry service."

Another well known family, the Luneys of Luney Construction, was always involved with annual Langford Lake regattas which Roberta described:

"Regattas were held at the lake every summer. Families often gathered at the Luney's cottage on Leigh Road to watch the events, relaxing in the shade on an awning-covered platform. There were benches against low walls where guests could watch swimming and boating and summer games including horseshoes, water ball, croquet and badminton.

"The platform was also the dance floor the night of the regatta, lit by Japanese lanterns and sometimes automobile headlights to augment the illumination. Everyone looked forward to bountiful refreshments, contributed by all the cottage families

"Many events started from the small island about halfway along the lake on the Goldstream Avenue [highway] side, as did the distance swim across the lake. Of course the swimmers were accompanied by several boats and ended near the railway tracks.

A Model T Ford, the Basustow family's first motor car transportation to the lake.

"The rowboat race began near the end of the lake and ended at the small island. It was for couples, the man rowing. My Dad and I usually took part but I can't remember if we ever won. Short races ended at the Bennett family's tea room near the small island. Tragically, a swimmer died one year near enough to the beach for spectators to wade out, but it was too late.

"At times during the summer it was so quiet around that lake that if you slammed a board onto a float just at dusk fish would jump all over the lake. My Dad used to love to prove to doubting visitors that he wasn't exaggerating when he told them about it. There were bass, catfish and sunfish in the lake then, but no trout."

Charles Basustow and his brother-in-law Robert Campbell of Portland, Oregon, sailing to home beach, sometime in the 1920s.
(Roberta Basustow Jones photos)

Cottage summers came to an end for Roberta's family after a tragedy in the winter of 1936. Her cousin's husband, Harry Green, drowned during a skating party as the skaters were taking "one last turn" around the lake. There were thin spots near the railway tracks where 'Hy' Green went through and was unable to surface through thick ice surrounding the thin patches. Another drowning victim the same evening was Jessie Alexander who was celebrating her engagement with another skating party. The tragedy merited an eight-column story on the front page of the Victoria Daily Times on February 19, 1936: Bodies of Drowned Skaters Recovered.

Hughes Family

Mary and Leslie Hughes with their eldest daughter Val choosing a site for the Langford Lake home in 1934. (Hughes family photo)

Leslie and Mary (Rockingham) Hughes bought land at Langford Lake in 1934, after several years in South America where Leslie worked for one of the cable companies. In a recent conversation 97-year-old Mary spoke of the contrast between her Rio de Janeiro home across from the famous Copacabana beach and the wooded property on which they built their Langford home, Bush Hill.

"My husband and my father both worked for the cable companies, and I met Leslie when they were both at work on a Caribbean station. We were married in 1930 at Christ Church Cathedral in Victoria and had a wonderful time living in Brazil until Leslie lost his job at the height of the Depression in 1933."

Their eldest daughter, Val, remembers that her father did a lot of the work building the house on the hill at Langford Lake where her sister Christine was born. "My parents bought two small waterside cottages as rental properties. One of these had been built by a sea captain in the form of a boat with rims around the counters. On the lower level there were built-in bunks ideal for visiting children. There was a float and a row boat, and I learned to row when I was about 5."

Val also remembers spending a lot of time with her Rockingham grandparents at the house on Millstream, walking miles over the old logging roads of Langford and the Highlands. She attended Langford Elementary School before her father was recalled to the cable station at Bamfield, the Vancouver Island terminus of the Pacific cable to Australia, an essential communications link in World War II. Her sister Alison was born there.

Their mother Mary continued to live in Port Alberni until the age of 96 when she moved back to the Langford area in 2002, near Alison's home on Goldstream Avenues. She often walks a mile each way to her daughter's home to paint at the little studio set up for her there. Alison Gardner is a travel writer and editor of a travel magazine.

Bush Hill, completed in 1935 on a hill across from Langford Lake, is still recognizable under a coat of stucco. (Hughes family photo)

Other Residents

Former newspaper writer and editor Alec Merriman lives on a rise above Langford Lake in one of the few remaining original bungalows. He has known the lake from childhood when his father took him fishing in boats rented at Bennett's Lakeshore Pavilion. The resort boasted a high diving board and a row of bath houses with changing booths facing the lake. Henry (Hank) Bennett was a good enough tennis player to try out for Canada's Davis Cup Team. Roberta Jones remembered Mrs. Bennett as a great golfer, often mentioned as a winner in newspaper accounts almost to the day of her death. The Bennett children were Pamela, Cecily and Henry. [2]

There was also a dance hall at the resort. In September, 1931, badminton players met at Langford Lakeside to form a club with Ernest LeQuesne as first president, Roland Jones, vice president and Mrs. H. A. Hincks secretary-treasurer. Miss G. Jones and H.C.C. Bennett were on the executive committee.

Times newspaper editor Benny Nicholas rented a lakeside cottage from the Peden family for several summers and made it available to reporters' families for holidays. There were some internationally known guests at the cottages too. Circus owner Clyde Beatty used to relax there when the circus was in town, and former British Prime Minister Clement Atlee came to tea at a Leigh Road cottage.

Most of the cottages are either gone or enlarged beyond recognition, turned into year-round homes much grander than the little summer camps. The older houses can be identified by their river rock chimneys. Members of the LeQuesne family still live on property bought by Kitty and Ernie LeQuesne after World War II.

The District of Langford has two scenic walkways at the lake. One runs parallel to the railway tracks south of the lake across wetlands and the gravel pit to the west. Another leads to the west end of the lake from Goldstream/The Highway. Selby Park is a small green space beside the highway near Leigh Road. The rest of the lakeshore is surrounded by privately owned homes.

Circus owner Clyde Beatty used to relax there when the circus was in town, and former British Prime Minister Clement Atlee came to tea at a Leigh Road cottage.

GLEN LAKE

Glen Lake, less than a mile south-east of Langford Lake at their closest points, was hidden behind an inaccessible wilderness enjoyed only by hunters and fishermen in early days. As more farms were established in the Happy Valley and Luxton areas, and a second railway line was proposed, lakefront property values rose and large landowners like Charles Pooley and A. R. Luxton felt it was time to promote residential development.

---

2   Sergeant Pamela Bennett, # 11 Bomber Reconnaissance Squadron, RCAF, died in a plane crash near Barkley Sound towards the end of World War II while on a routine trip to familiarize the seven-man crew with local airfields.

A 1911 subdivision plan shows long narrow lots radiating out from Glen Lake to a road encircling the development. Lots varied in size and price from just over an acre for $500 to more than three acres for as much as $1,200. Lot 16, five and a half acres at the west end of the lake, was a whopping $2,000. The developers promoted the lots as ideal for country summer houses, with splendid views and attractive surroundings. The soil, they claimed, was suitable for fruit growing.

The four-acre site at the south east corner of the lake, near the railway to Sooke and beyond, was reserved for a train station, hotel and general store with post office. The Glen Lake Hotel is still there near the Happy Valley Road intersection. The rail line which once transported timber from Lake Cowichan and passengers to and from the city, is now part of the regional linear park known as the Galloping Goose trail.

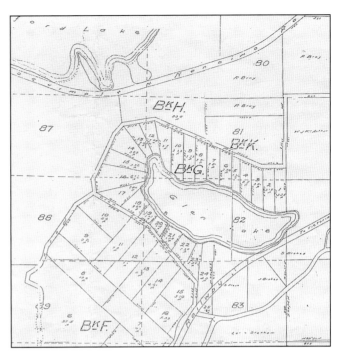

Subdivision plan for summer cottages at Glen Lake left a four-acre site for a hotel, train station, store and post office

A steam locomotive near Glen Lake.
(Elwood White photo)

Boys on raft at Glen Lake (Dorothy Blenkinsop photo)

FLORENCE LAKE

Florence Lake, the smallest of Langford's three lakes, is less than a mile north of the Trans Canada Highway and is the least well-known. Skirt Mountain, with its old copper mining sites, and the nearby Miniskirt, loom over the lake from the northwest.

Hazel Olson remembered that her father used to hunt there and that it was a favourite hiking and picnic area for her family between 1910 and 1920 before the Trans Canada Highway blocked off the trails to the lake from their Millstream Road homes. Her husband and father logged parts of the mountain and "supplied hundreds of cords of fuel wood for the hungry greenhouse heating plant and its tireless belching chimney" that William Savory built in 1910.

Axel Olson and his brother-in-law Vollie McTavish logged parts of Skirt Mountain in 1921 and 1922. They rafted the logs across Florence lake on the 'Ogopogo' then trucked them to the log dump at Parson's Bridge and eventually to the Wilfert Mill across Esquimalt Harbour. (Scafe/Wale photo)

Savory Family

The Savory family lived in Victoria's Fernwood district when they first arrived from England. "They had several large greenhouses there to supply their seed and produce store at the corner of Broad and Fort Streets. By 1910 Savory realized that his [Fernwood] property would be totally inadequate for the expansion plans he envisioned, so he purchased 200 gravelly acres in Langford. Here he moved his family, including daughter Lillian and sons William, Fred and George, into a comfortable home adjoining a group of large greenhouses. A huge brick chimney plant provided heat for tomato plants and a great variety of nursery shrubs and trees. The chimney became something of a landmark near Savory Road over the next 60 years.

"In spite of long days and tiring work, Savory continued to operate two businesses, travelling daily from Langford to his Victoria sales outlet. It wasn't long before the Savorys found room on their property for the first Langford Gun Club. William Savory joined the 5th Volunteer Regiment and became a gunner-buddy of my father." (Hazel Olson memoirs)

Their daughter, Miss Lillian Savory, was such a well known community personality that she became

George Newham and Axel Olson at the Scafe/Olson logging operation at Florence Lake. Vollie McTavish's son Arthur confirms there was also a woodcutting operation and a small sawmill later at the north east end of the lake. (Scafe/Wale photos)

'The Grand Old Lady of Langford." She was active in many Langford associations, including the Women's Institutes, the Luxton Fair, the National Council of Women and church organizations. When the South Vancouver Island District women's institutes held an international picnic in Beacon Hill Park one summer Miss Savory made corsages for all the delegates in the Institute colours of green, gold and white. Her hospitality was extended to visiting dignitaries and local community workers, and her name appears in many competitions at flower shows and fairs. Even when she had a leg amputated in later years she continued to attend all the functions to which she was invited. Miss Lillian died in 1972 in her 93rd year. Savory Elementary School on Atkins Road is named in her honour.

Strachans and other families

Jean Strachan of Setchfield Road, formerly Florence Lake Road, remembers the east side of the lake in 1942 when the only permanent residents were the Beans, Stubbs, Spencers and the Strachans. Mr. and Mrs. Bean and their son Charlie lived at the south end of the lake when Jean and Pat Strachan arrived to live in what had been a tourist cabin. The Stubbs lived next door, first in the garage while building the main house. One winter the lake rose so high that it crossed the road and a fair-sized front garden right into the garage where they were still living with their young son and daughter. The Spencers had a small store and kept some row boats for hire.

Roy and Frank Bigelow and their elderly parents moved to the large area which is now the trailer court. Ed Cushing came a little later, leaving his wife and two little girls in Winnipeg while he

One winter the lake rose so high that it crossed the road and a fair-sized front garden right into the garage...

Members of the James Bay Athletic Association hired this horse-drawn car from the Victoria Transfer Company to take them to Florence Lake for a picnic in the early 1900s. (BC Archives A-02797)

enlarged the house high on a rock south of the Strachans. He spent the summer building a room below the cottage pecking away at the rock all summer with chisel and hammer.

There were a few cottages on the west side of the lake but there was no access by road. An unconfirmed rumour has it that someone living on that side of the lake tried to transport a grand piano across the lake but the boat capsized. The piano may still be at the bottom of the lake, according to the story. One cottage burned to the ground but the fire department could do nothing. Even if they had been able to cross the lake there was no water supply.

In fact there were no utilities. There were no houses between the small lakeside community and Langford School beside the Speedway. Before the Trans Canada highway was built the Strachans and their neighbours used to walk to the trolley diner for supplies, mail and newspapers. They had to pay the milkman, Mr. Hincks, an extra two cents for bottles broken on the terrible road.

Jean Strachan's most vivid memory of the terrible road is the harrowing night time drive to the hospital to give birth to her daughter Carol in 1943. The car hit the stump that rose up in the middle of the road every winter when rain washed away the gravel around it, but the damage to the car was slight and Pat Strachan drove his wife to the hospital in time. The road was improved shortly after this and the stump never rose up out of the road bed again.

The District of Langford has built a public walkway partly around the east side and the southern end of the lake from Florence Lake Road, but the surrounding land is almost all privately owned.

Who Was Florence?

There is a mystery about how the lake got its name. First choice for some is Florence Dumbleton, the wife of Henry Dumbleton, thought to be the first settlers in the area. Census records show they came to Canada in 1889 and bought property near Skirt Mountain and the lake. They are better known for their house called Rockland which gave its name to Victoria's grandest neighbourhood and to the street formerly known as Belcher Road

Florence Savory, wife of William Savory whose nursery and greenhouses were on the west side of the lake along Savory Road at the Trans Canada Highway (which didn't exist then) is another possibility. Savory Road used to be called Muir Road, so perhaps there was a Florence Muir too. James Phair's daughter Florence, born at Goldstream in 1886, also has a connection with the area close to her father's copper mining operation. Others say it was named as long ago as the 1850s after Captain Langford's daughter Florence, but the lake is not shown on 1850s maps. So far, Florence Dumbleton has the majority vote.

PARKS

In addition to its own parks and walking trails The District of Langford has Provincial and Regional Parks within its boundaries. The best known, Goldstream Provincial Park near Langford's northern boundary, was turned over to the Province by the City of Victoria in 1958. A section of the Galloping Goose trail along the former Canadian National Railway right-of-way through Langford is part of the Capital Regional District's linear park. Mill Hill park came under the jurisdiction of the CRD in 1981.

The Cedar Grove Tea Room was a popular place at Goldstream Flats until after World War II. (Goldstream Museum)

Goldstream Park

The City of Victoria owned Goldstream Park as part of its Sooke/Goldstream watershed system during the first half of the 20th century until the Capital Regional District was put in charge of water management. In the late 1930s and through World War II the city

Goldstream Park, renowned for its huge old growth trees and the annual return of salmon to the Goldstream River spawning grounds, has been popular with Victorians and visitors for more than 100 years. This well-dressed picnic group photographed in the 1890s would recognize the forest scene even now. (BC Archives B-02387)

also owned the Cedar Grove Tea Room, a log building with a large stone fire place nestled among the old growth forest on river flats.

The tea room had a huge stone fireplace at the north end, a door facing the road and another leading to a brick-trimmed cement patio facing the river. During the summer of 1942 it was also popular with several groups of soldiers camped on the flats en route from Nanaimo to a camp at Colwood. Five hundred members of The Rocky Mountain Rangers helped the young manager of the tea room, Helen Savoie, by chopping wood to keep the fireplace glowing. Later, 800 soldiers from the Victoria Rifles and the Royal rifles descended on the flats and enjoyed the wonderful lemon pies Helen and her mother served during their stay. (Helen Savoie article, Colonist Weekend Magazine, n.d.)

Lillian Gish and local extras on the Saanich Inlet set of the film "The Commandos Strike at Dawn". (Courtesy Pat Taylor)

The Goldstream Flats also served as a sort of staging ground for the extras in a morale-building wartime film called *The Commandos Strike at Dawn*. The 1942 movie was based on a story by C. S. Forester and starred Paul Muni with Anna Lee, Lillian Gish and Sir Cedric Hardwicke in supporting roles.

The site chosen was the Stacy's boat house, later Hall's and now the Goldstream Boat House, close to Langford's northern boundary about half way up the hill north of Goldstream Park. Just as the climb begins there is a narrow road to the right leading down to the boat house on the shores of Finlayson Arm. A 'Norwegian Village' set was built on and around the dock, and the Saanich Inlet served well as a Norwegian fiord. The commandos of the story included 100 soldiers, sailors and airmen from local units who camped in two large tents on Goldstream Flats during the filming.

Pat Taylor was one of the young dance students from the Wynne Shaw studio who acted as village school children in the film. "It was marvellous," Pat recalled. "We gathered at the Empress Hotel and were bussed out to the site where we were fed lavishly. The extras sat around a lot, but the excitement and the food made time pass quickly. We were supposed to look a bit grungy as we bravely sang

Program for the gala premiere of the film at the Capitol Theatre on December 17, 1942. Proceeds from the show were donated to "the welfare of the three services in the area," according to a note in the program by Air Vice Marshal L. F. Stevenson. Major General G. R. Pearkes, Commander-in-Chief, Pacific Command, wrote that local military personnel enjoyed their roles in the film. (Courtesy Pat Taylor)

the Norwegian national anthem in front of the school house and tried to raise the Norwegian flag. But the evil Nazis made us stop and raised the German swastika instead."

The filming was finished in town, probably at the Willows Fairgrounds, where Wynne Shaw had to teach the actors how to dance a polka. There were lots of local extras of all ages involved, including Pat's distinguished white-haired grandfather as a village dignitary.

Mill Hill Park

Mill Hill Regional Park begins where Millstream emerges from its underground channel at Atkins Road. The quiet trails wind from the banks of the stream to the 600-foot summit where a forest service lookout tower stood for nearly 40 years. Many years before European contact it was a hunting site for Coast Salish Indians who fished and hunted deer and elk in and around the Saanich Arm, now known as the Saanich Inlet.

A Millstream waterfall near the entrance to Mill Hill Park, one of Victoria's best kept secrets. Most weekdays, visitors are so scarce and the steep trails so quiet that it seems to be Langford's closest thing to the wilderness of a century ago.
(M. Duffus photo)

This 1860 watercolour is the only known image of the Hudson's Bay Company sawmill and gristmill at Millstream Falls at the head of Esquimalt Harbour. Midshipman Richard Frederick Britten of the Royal Navy painted the scene after he and a fellow officer rowed to the stream to collect fresh water for naval ships anchored across the harbour. (BC Archives PDP5438)

The park's apparently changeless character is misleading. In recent history it has been logged for the Hudson's Bay Company's 1848 mill (which gave the hill its name); it has been the site of a forest service lookout from 1935 to 1976, and a forest insect survey area for a few years after World War II.

HBC officer Roderick Finlayson's entries in the Fort Victoria Post Journal for 1848 are the first recorded descriptions of Millstream and Mill Hill. He had orders to find a source of water power for a saw mill and grist mill to supply the Fort and other paying customers. The mills were built at the head of Esquimalt Harbour, where Rowe's Stream (now Millstream) roared over a 20-foot ledge in an impressive waterfall in winter. Unfortunately the roar dwindled to a whispering trickle in summer when the ledge turned green with moss and ferns. The frustrated Mr. Finlayson set out to find an additional source of water farther upstream. His journal entries describe his two-day expedition with John Fenton, the millwright, and their Indian guides.

They explored "through the most rugged and forbidding country imaginable." They climbed what would later be called Mount Finlayson for a fine view of the Saanich Arm, and camped "near the source of Mill Stream." Next day they "struck across the valley behind the mill mountain" until they came to a large lake (later known as Thetis Lake) which they hoped would have outlets emptying into the Esquimalt Lagoon. Their search ended in disappointment.

The forest around Mill Hill supplied timber for the sawmill for the few years it operated. The sawmill and nearby grist mill were damaged beyond repair, washed away by an uncommonly rainy season in 1854.

A few settlers lived nearby, including some families once connected with the mill, like the Donald McKenzies. Half a century later Mill Hill was remembered by early Langford residents as a grand place for picnics and hunting. It was still known as Mill Mountain when the Scafe family and their friends used to hike to the summit for

Unfortunately the roar dwindled to a whispering trickle in summer when the ledge turned green with moss and ferns.

Forest Service tractor trailer at the Mill Hill fire suppression camp, shows an old orchard approximately on the site of the present parking lot. (BC Archives NA-07090)

One widespread rumour claims that the panoramic view of Esquimalt Harbour and the naval station made it a convenient lookout for German spies lurking atop the hill during World War II.

Summer jobs were much sought after by students from Victoria High School, The University of Victoria and The University of British Columbia.

picnics. One widespread rumour claims that the panoramic view of Esquimalt Harbour and the naval station made it a convenient lookout for German spies lurking atop the hill during World War II. No records have been found to substantiate the story.

Two government agencies occupied parts of the hill after World War II. The Provincial Forest Service first established a ranger station at its Langford headquarters in 1937. The Rangers were responsible for fire suppression in a large area of southern Vancouver Island from Port Renfrew to Mill Bay on the east shore of the Saanich Inlet. The lookout on Mill Hill was one of three watch towers maintained by the service until the early 1970s.

The Federal Department of Agriculture leased land at Mill Hill from the provincial government for its forest insect survey. According to Chief Scientist Dave Evans, who ran the field station at the foot of Mill Hill from 1949 to 1965, the department was interested in the study of insects to be used for biological control. Buildings included a research facility, office, house, and a storage shed approximately where CRD Parks headquarters is now located. Summer jobs were much sought after by students from Victoria High School, The University of Victoria and The University of British Columbia. When the Pacific Forest Centre was built in 1965 the Mill Hill facility was turned over to Langford. (Cited in CRD history of Mill Hill Park)

A fire suppression crew used the old federal buildings in the summer fire season until 1976. In 1980 the old federal building became the Capital Regional District Parks office, but by 1990 it was in such poor shape that renovations were abandoned and it was torn down The old operations building was modified to provide extra storage and office space until the new Parks Administration building was completed.

The rocky roads that led up the hill to bring food and supplies to the lookout tower have reverted to walking trails, providing a serious hike to the summit but a gentle stroll along the lower trails east of Millstream. The magnificent view of Esquimalt Harbour and a scenic panorama of Victoria make the climb to the summit well worth while. Many of the surrounding hill tops are identified by a peak-finder cairn on the site of the old lookout towers.

Residential development has crept up the sides of the hill, but the 50 hectare strip of park shown on the map preserves at least a section of the hill, now connected by a rugged trail on the east side of the hill to the 50 hectare Thetis Lake regional park (across the Trans Canada Highway), and from Thetis to the Francis King park in Saanich.

Photographs by Ron Jones, who was in charge of the Langford Ranger Station from 1958 to 1967, were taken as the lookout tower was being pulled down for safety reasons. The 50-foot high wooden-beam structure, which once had telephone and radio connections to the central station in Langford, resisted strongly to being toppled.

11

ORGANIZATIONS AND ATTRACTIONS

LANGFORD VOLUNTEER FIRE DEPARTMENT

As in all rural communities fires in the woods and dry grass in the summer, overheated wood stoves and fireplaces in the winter, kept Langford residents watchful and ready to act. They were on their own in the early days, relying on neighbours and occasional help from the Forest Service who conscripted local men to help at 25 to 30 cents an hour.

Rural fire protection districts were organized during World War II as A.R.P. (Air Raid Precaution) units trained under a civil defense program. After the war Langford, View Royal and Colwood formed separate volunteer fire departments.

The Langford Community Club took over operation of the volunteer department in 1945 and bought the disbanded A.R.P.equipment for $1. The basement of the new community hall at the corner of Goldstream and Carlow roads served as the first fire hall. In January, 1947, the ratepayers of Langford formed a Fire Protection District under the Provincial Water Act. Rodney Bayles, son of wartime fire warden A. F. Bayles, was the first volunteer fire chief.

Langford's first fire truck – a 1926 Chevrolet. (Langford Fire Department)

The 1948 Dodge truck was too big for the Community Hall basement. (Langford Fire Department)

Austin Yates donated the land for first firehall in 1950. Back of the Yates house can be seen at right rear.
(Langford Fire Department)

The spectacular Olson sawmill fire, 1952, was next to the "new" firehall. (Langford Fire Department)

There were approximately 20 volunteers. The first fire truck was a 1926 Chevrolet truck acquired from a Chinese vegetable gardener. Water was carried in barrels in the back as there was no pump or hose. Volunteer firemen and others built a 500-gallon-a-minute pumper to the specifications of the B.C. Fire Underwriters, and in 1948 bought a new two-ton Dodge pickup truck to transport it. The new truck was too big for the Community Hall basement.

The first purpose-built firehall was begun in 1950 on land donated by Austin Yates in memory of his parents, Mr. and Mrs. James Stuart Yates. The new station was built by volunteers on what had been the paddock at the back of the Goldstream Avenue property. The hall had two bays, an office, a spare room and a hose tower.

In 1952 the community raised money to buy a pumper truck and a newer ambulance from the Saanich Fire Department. In 1958 a 2000-gallon tanker truck, the biggest tanker in the Province, was the pride of the department.

Rod Bayles was hired as first full time fire chief in 1955. Other early chiefs were Dave Smith and Ritchie LeQuesne, whose younger brother Allan served as chief for 33 years from 1961, 30 of them as paid fire chief from 1967.

Allan LeQuesne joined as a volunteer in 1952. On his first day at work the Highway Sawmill on the Olson property on Goldstream Avenue burned to the ground in a spectacular blaze. Later as Langford's fire chief he was in charge during several other memorable fires, including 'the big fire' at the Luxton fair grounds and the demise of the venerable Gaucher building in 1972.

The Goldstream Avenue hall served the entire district until 1964 when a second hall was built on Happy Valley Road. A new main hall was completed on Millstream Avenue in 1975, replacing the first building which still stands. A third hall was built on Sooke Lake Road in 1984 to serve the Goldstream area.

At time of writing the large new state-of-the-art hall on Millstream Road just south of the Trans Canada Highway serves as Langford headquarters. The earlier Millstream Road hall was torn down and the property sold to make way for commercial establishments.

The Women's Auxiliary.

Wives of the firemen and other community volunteers have been organizing fund-raising events since the early 1950s. Proceeds from dances, luncheons, teas, bake sales, fashion shows, craft and jewelry parties contributed to many fire department projects. These included purchase of equipment for the Western Communities ambulance when it was operated by the Langford Fire department. Special telephones for the deaf purchased for the emergency fire services were later donated to the RCMP communication centre.

Members have provided hundreds of snacks and meals at all hours of day or night for on-duty firemen and rescue crews, especially during forest fire seasons when the Langford firefighters worked with the Forest Service fire suppression crews. They have also published three cook books featuring recipes contributed by wives of firemen and auxiliary members as fund raisers. The Auxiliary sponsors a Junior Citizenship Award trophy for deserving students of Belmont School.

Fire Chief Allan LeQuesne

PRINCE EDWARD BRANCH, #91, ROYAL CANADIAN LEGION

(Condensed from research by Wallace Klages.)

As in hundreds of communities across Canada after the First World War, Langford veterans formed a branch of the Canadian Legion of the British Empire Service League. Prince Edward Branch #91 received its charter on September 1, 1927. Sergeant Major

Early meetings were held in a small clubhouse on property belonging to the Savory family.

Alexander Gowans Mackie was instrumental in its formation, and served as its first president.

Early meetings were held in a small clubhouse on property belonging to the Savory family. Sparse records from the early years mention masquerade dances and New Years' Eve events in the Colwood Women's Institute Hall, rented for $10 for the evening.

The second clubhouse was the Gaucher building, purchased from the LeQuesne brothers. The old dance hall on the upper floor served as the Legion Hall. After renovations were made in the late 1930s the lower floor was rented out as office space. That was the year of the first recorded church parade from the post office to St. Matthew's Church. The first woman member, Megan Williams, joined in 1945.

The next move was to 940 Dunford Avenue, using a hut from the Colwood army camp as clubhouse. Membership dwindled to the point where there was talk of relinquishing the charter, but younger veterans joined to help with renovations at the club and membership grew as monthly meetings continued. An entertainment committee organized dinners, dances and parties as fundraisers. Older members were well cared for when they were sick or needed transportation or other assistance. An addition to the building was completed by 1960. Cy Price nights became annual events thanks to the owner of Price's store, a generous contributor to the building fund.

The Cenotaph of the Prince Edward Branch of the Canadian Legion led a peripatetic life before this new memorial was installed at Veterans' Memorial Park in October, 2001. In various forms it has followed the branch from the first clubhouse on the Savory property to the Gaucher building on Goldstream, an army hut on Dunford Road, and to the Juan de Fuca Centennial Park. The new cenotaph, representing a grieving mother, was designed and built by Langford sculptor Derek Rowe with his assistant Chris Hess.
(M. Duffus photo)

The move to 761 Station Avenue on property acquired from Walter Scotney brought the branch to its present location. Lieutenant Governor George Pearkes officially opened the new building on February 19, 1964. It now has a lounge, an auditorium, a games room and kitchen. An Honour Roll listing local residents who lost their lives in World Wars I and II was unveiled in 1994. Names of local men and women who enlisted in Canadian armed forces are listed on scrolls mounted on a Wall of Remembrance in the lounge.

The building also houses several active community organizations including the Goldstream Food Bank Society, the Western Community Christmas Hamper Fund, Langford Emergency Social Services, Metchosin and South Vancouver Island Lions Clubs, Boy Scouts, Girl Guides, cadets and many sports teams.

Bursaries and scholarship funds provide financial assistance to graduating students of Belmont Senior Secondary School as well as bursaries for adults upgrading their education. Prince Edward Lodge, a low rental residence, was built in 1976 on adjoining property on Station Road.

Outstanding Canadian World War I hero Sir Arthur Currie is the young officer fourth from left, second row, in this photograph of Victoria's Fifth Militia taken June 10, 1904, on the Langford Plains, now part of the Royal Colwood Golf Club. He led Canadian soldiers in the capture of Vimy Ridge in April, 1917. This breakthrough earned the former Victoria school teacher, realtor and insurance salesman a knighthood and promotion to Lieutenant General to command the Canadian Corps. A stone from Vimy Ridge at the base of the Langford cenotaph holds a plaque commemorating the famous battle. (City of Vancouver Archives, LP236. Photograph by `Jones')

Alexander Gowans Mackie, a much decorated soldier, was well known in Langford as Langford Station Postmaster from 1919 to 1945, and the proprietor of Mackie's Grocery Store near the E.&N. station. He was born at Woolwich, Kent, in 1870 and emigrated to Canada with his wife, Alice, after the First World War. He served in the Imperial Army with the Royal Horse Artillery for 19 years, and with the Light Horse for four. He was appointed Battalion Sergeant Major at Valcartier in August, 1914, promoted to Warrant Officer on September 9, and enlisted in the 5th battalion, Canadian Expeditionary Force, on September 22. He was Mentioned in Despatches in December, 1915, and awarded the Distinguished Conduct Medal the following June. He was given an honourable discharge from the Army on compassionate grounds on May 12, 1917, to take up residence in Saskatchewan Landing, Saskatchewan.

Mrs. Mackie, who was born in Steeples, England, in 1870, played a leading role in the Ladies Auxiliary to the Legion Branch and many other Langford activities. She died in January, 1954, and is buried in Hatley Memorial Gardens beside her husband, who died in February, 1947. (From research by Wallace Klages)

(Records of Langford residents who served in World Wars I and II have been meticulously researched by Wallace Klages and printed in his 1999 Book of Remembrance. Langford servicemen killed in World War I included Percival Archie Corry, James Arthur Dixon, Bertram Hincks, William Dumbleton Holmes and Henry Halwood Neild. World War II casualties included Pamela Bennett, William Fitzherbert Bullen, Claude Harvey Hincks, Harold Keith Langrish and Michael Richard Frewin Oliver.)

THE FARMERS' AND WOMEN'S INSTITUTES

It is unlikely that anyone ever reached upper income brackets from farming in Langford. Crops were grown and livestock raised in Langford's rural days, but mostly on small parcels of land and with great difficulty. Chicken ranching and greenhouse nurseries proved more profitable. Chinese vegetable farms and a dairy farm did well between Langford Lake and Dewdney Flats, in spite of winter floods.

Agricultural problems were uppermost for the early settlers in 1898 when the first Farmers' Institute in British Columbia was formed. Farmers in what was then called the Esquimalt District sent a petition to the Provincial Government requesting some kind of committee to deal specifically with agricultural questions. Deputy Minister of Agriculture J. R. Anderson invited farmers from all over B.C. to a meeting in Victoria in 1897 to discuss the farmers' institute

One of its first objectives was to attract further permanent settlement by improving conditions of rural life.

movement in Ontario as a possible model. The result was the Metchosin Farmers' Institute, incorporated on December 1, 1898, with members from Parson's Bridge to Rocky Point, including Langford, Goldstream, Colwood, Metchosin, Sooke and the Highlands.

One of its first objectives was to attract further permanent settlement by improving conditions of rural life. Goals included greater crop yields per acre, better farm management, more efficient business methods and marketing.

Demonstration plots were planted with varieties of crops to see which would perform best under local conditions. Other plots were used to demonstrate different types of fertilizers. Livestock and poultry stock were improved with high-quality breeding stock introduced by the government, whose representatives were available for advice and lectures.

The Institute was registered under the Agricultural Associations Act in 1914, and its advisory board met with the Minister of Agriculture annually to discuss concerns and make recommendations.

Membership lapsed during the depression when farmers were unable to sell their produce and gave up on their farms. Those who remained regrouped after World War II when former service personnel returned to farming with assistance from the Veterans Land Act, successor to the Soldiers Settlement Board. Results were far from promising.

Since then Langford has succumbed to the pressure of development and there's hardly a cow or chicken to be seen in suburbia. The Farmers' Institute still sponsors an agricultural fair on the Luxton Fair grounds purchased in 1928. A major attraction is the display of antique farm machinery collected and restored by members of the Institute. A heritage display now recognizes the early farming and logging families and a way of life that has passed into history.

(Much of the information about the early days is from Alan Littler's History of the Metchosin Farmers' Institute. He lists some early directors including W. H. Hayward, John Wallace, T. Oldershaw, G. Heatherbell, W. O. Sweatman and C. E. Whitney-Griffiths. Secretary-treasurer from 1919 to 1921 was A. Hankin, whose granddaughter, Lynda Dowling, and her husband reside on her grandfather's property, now the Happy Valley Lavender and Herbs Farm)

Membership lapsed during the depression when farmers were unable to sell their produce and gave up on their farms.

A heritage display now recognizes the early farming and logging families and a way of life that has passed

Langford Women's Institute

The Women's Institute movement was also concerned with agriculture when farmers' wives were often in charge of the poultry and dairy products. Improvement of flocks and advice about butter and cheese-making were part of the W.I. programs in most communities. Emphasis was also on helping country wives with domestic as well as farm activities. The Langford Women's Institute was formed in 1914, two months before the start of World War I. The Happy Valley Women's Institute first met in 1924.

The first meeting of the Langford Women's Institute was held June 8, 1914, and the first item of business was to affiliate with the Society for the Prevention of the Mortality of Infants, one of the earliest causes taken up by the Women's Institute movement when it was formed in Ontario in 1897.

Over the years Langford members did much more to fulfill the needs of their community. They held domestic science and dressmaking classes, and arranged for a VON nurse (Victorian Order of Nurses) for the district. They were active in the Red Cross during

Langford Women's Institute members at their hall on Dunford Road, ca. 1936. Miss Lillian Savory is recognizable as the tiny woman third from right in the front row. Mrs. Bullen was president for 20 years. (Goldstream Museum)

World War 1, and sent 60 plum puddings, cooked in the large ovens at Savory nurseries, to Britain for one wartime Christmas.

They worked with ministers of education and agriculture for improved schools and better farming and gardening methods. Langford members worked zealously with other South Vancouver Island Institutes for the Queen Alexandra Solarium. They also started a children's library and gave school prizes.

An Institute course of 10 lessons in parliamentary procedure and standing committees was well attended, as were most W.I. procedural courses. The courses were designed to give women a better chance to make their voices heard – and listened to – beyond home and school. Mrs. E. H. Phipps and Mrs. A. L Gordon represented Langford at the first provincial conference in 1924. Although its membership is smaller now, members of the Langford W.I. still work with other South Vancouver Island Institutes on one of their original projects, the Queen Alexandra Foundation.

A major fund-raising effort made it possible for the Langford W.I. to buy 1.5 acres of land for $184.08, for their hall on Dunford Road, left. A housing development now on the site acknowledged the Women's Institute movement by naming it Adelaide Village, in honour of W.I. founder Adelaide Hoodless. (Goldstream Museum)

Source: Modern Pioneers, British Columbia Women's Institute, 1909 – 1959. Editor Gillian Douglas. Evergreen Press Ltd. Many well known Langford members are listed, including Miss Lillian Savory, Mrs. Percy Welch, Mrs. J. Dewar, Mrs. D. B. F. Bullen, Mrs. H. Hincks, Mrs. F. Staverman, Mrs. R. Carlow and Mrs. S. Hutchinson

Happy Valley And Luxton Women's Institute

The first meeting of the Happy Valley Women's Institute was held January 22, 1924, in the Happy Valley (later Luxton) Community Hall. In addition to homemaking projects members worked for repairs and improvements to the hall, improved mail and bus service, lower electricity rates, road safety and Bilston Creek improvement. They also held classes in tree pruning, the first in B.C.

Mrs. Mary Cooper received the first life membership in 1925. Members regularly sent donations of eggs, fruit and jams to the Queen Alexandra Solarium, and donated an encyclopedia to Belmont School.

On May 12, 1937, they planted a seedling oak in the Happy Valley schoolyard to commemorate the coronation of King George

They were active in the Red Cross during World War 1, and sent 60 plum puddings, cooked in the large ovens at Savory nurseries, to Britain for one wartime Christmas.

VI and Queen Elizabeth. The Happy Valley Institute is no longer in existence.

The Women's Institutes movement was started by Adelaide Hoodless, founder of the first Women's Institute in the world at Stoney Creek, Ontario, in 1897. The purpose was to improve the life of women in rural communities, something like the women's equivalent of the farmers' institutes. If farmers' institutes could help men raise better crops an institute for women could help in the even more important work of raising better families.

The movement spread across Canada to the United States by 1912, then to Britain. Mrs. Alfred Watt of Metchosin introduced the Institute idea to the British Isles and formed the first W.I. on the island of Anglesey in Wales, modeling it on those of British Columbia. The idea spread "like fire before a gale." Queen Mary invited Mrs. Watt to go to Sandringham to explain the movement. The Sandringham W.I. was formed with the Queen as president. Queen Elizabeth the Queen Mother was still president of the Sandringham W.I. until her death in 2002. During the First World War the efforts of British countrywomen increased the food supply by between 35 to 60 per cent and the Institutes became known as Canada's gift to the motherland. For her services Mrs. Watt was awarded the Order of the British Empire by King George V. She returned to Victoria and was a frequent guest of local Institutes.

THE PRIORY HOSPITAL

The Sisters of the Love of Jesus, under the direction of Mother Cecilia Mary, opened St. Mary's Priory in 1951 on land purchased from the Royal Colwood Golf and Country Club, once part of Captain Langford's farm. The Club's administration building was renovated to house the first 66 elderly residents in need of long term care. The first unit of the hospital was officially opened in March, 1953, by Bishop J. M. Hill, with Mayor Claude Harrison of Victoria in attendance.

The Sisters saw the need for an extended care facility and awarded a contract to build the additional facilities to the Scafe brothers, Robert and David. Cost of the 24-bed hospital was a remarkably low $65,000. The community welcomed the new facility operated by the Sisters in conjunction with the British Columbia Hospital Insurance Service. More space was soon added and the 71-unit addition was known as The House of Peace.

Eventually the administration of the growing hospital became too much for the Sisters, who found it difficult to recruit younger women to the Order. Problems were outlined at a public meeting by Dr. Embert VanTilburg, chairman of the Priory Hospital Board; hospital administrator George Harrison, Sister Elizabeth and Mother Ferdinand. The result was a transfer of responsibilities to a new administrative body, the Juan de Fuca Hospital Board. Mother Cecelia left to start a controversial animal shelter near the Malahat and Dr. Van Tilburg became Executive Director of St. Joseph's Hospital in Victoria. His contribution to the Langford facility over many years is remembered gratefully by the community.

The Priory Hospital was one of the first nursing homes to come under the Ministry of Health as an extended care hospital. It emphasizes a home-like atmosphere for residents, and its fame has spread since Maclean's Magazine published a photograph in June, 2000, showing the Priory's therapy garden near the new buildings.

SOUTH VANCOUVER ISLAND RANGERS

The Ranger story is condensed from booklets published to mark various anniversaries of the group since its formation in 1947. The clubhouse and extensive park grounds are on Lippincott Road.

Originally the Ranger organization consisted of a voluntary group of woodsmen who guarded the unprotected watersheds that supplied water and power to greater Victoria during World War II. Members served under the B.C. Provincial Police, and for a time were part of the Pacific Coast Militia Rangers. They patrolled and guarded the security of a large area from Shawnigan and the Koksilah River through to Sombrio Point on the West Coast, to Langford and part of the Highlands District.

After the war other organizations were responsible for security, but former Rangers were still called on by provincial and municipal police to assist in missing person incidents. A group of former rangers, concerned that such a useful organization might disappear, formed the South Vancouver Island Rangers Inc. in July, 1947. Its

Members served under the B.C. Provincial Police, and for a time were part of the Pacific Coast Militia Rangers.

...a voluntary group of woodsmen who guarded the unprotected watersheds that supplied water and power to greater Victoria during World War II.

Tracking dogs were trained and kept for many years before B.C. police forces worked with dogs.

objectives were to foster ranger training for the younger generation, to encourage healthy activities and sportsmanship, and to continue the volunteer Ranger Emergency Service. The service functioned only under the authority of the police, game branch or forestry officers, and never took part in any criminal case. Neither the organization nor any Ranger has ever accepted payment for services.

Tracking dogs were trained and kept for many years before B.C. police forces worked with dogs. Ranger dogs were sent to search for lost persons as far away as Cortez Island and Kelowna, but most cases were within an 80-mile radius of Victoria.

The Rangers maintained two fully equipped ambulances, the services of two registered nurses – wives of Rangers – who supplied medication and oxygen if needed. A trailer-type field kitchen, radio communications car, mobile unit telephone and portable stretcher, snowshoes, toboggan and alpine ropes were ready for rescue all year round. A five-passenger seaplane and two ocean going diesel craft, owned by individual rangers, were also available for rescue service.

Publicity given to the Ranger Emergency Service brought requests for information from similar groups in Canada, the U.S., South America and Australia. The need for this service ended after police, fire department and hospitals provided emergency services to Langford and other rural areas.

The group still maintains the parkland property known as the Ranger Club Grounds on Lippincott Road.

THE LANGFORD SPEEDWAY

The first race at Jack Taylor's gravel track near his garage on the Old Island Highway was held on June 6, 1936. It was the first auto-racing track in the area, located on a 10-acre property adjacent to Jack's own land and the Langford Elementary School. Local sawmill owner Axel Olson supplied lumber for fencing, booths and bleachers, and the secretary of the Vancouver Island Tourist Trade and Development Association officiated at the opening of the track.

Three thousand gallons of oil were reportedly poured over the 3/10 of a mile track to keep down the dust, and the cars were started by rope tow or a push start. The program attracted several American entries including the northwest champion, Jimmy Wilburn from

Jack Taylor, of Taylor's garage and the Langford Speedway.
(Scafe/Wale Photo)

Early race cars and a crash through the fence at Langford Speedway
(Speedway Scrapbook collection)

Seattle. Local drivers included Jimmy Logie, and Ed Allen. The last race of the evening was a 30-lap open event enjoyed by 2000 spectators in spite of the choking dust and flying rocks. The track was blacktopped for the 1937 season and lights were installed for night racing.

Faster cars increased the possibility of accidents by the 1938 season. A newspaper article listed safety concerns and urged race officials to have an ambulance or properly equipped crash car available for quick transportation to hospital.

Novelty events included a Model T race. Local owner Ken Hincks won one of the first races. Novelty bicycle races also became popular.

Racing continued during the first two years of World War II until wasting rationed gasoline for racecars was severely criticized. After the war a new grandstand seating 1,000 more racing enthusiasts was built and an electronic eye replaced the old-fashioned flag for time trials. The first Miss Speedway Queen contest was held, and the popular Victoria musical group, The Hometowners, performed their song "Langford Speedway Blues" during an intermission.

Racing at the Langford Speedway ended in 1949. Overcrowding and proximity to the school added to safety concerns. With no land available for expansion speedway owner Bruce Passmore sold the 10-acre site to the Sooke School District. Langford Elementary

Andy Cottyn completed the Western Speedway, a small half-mile flat dirt auto speedway, almost single handedly in less than a year. There were parking places for 2000 cars and grandstand seating for 3500 spectators. The races are still a major Langford summer attraction.

became the only school in the province with a 3/10 mile track and bleachers for track sports.

The Western Speedway on Millstream Road near the Langford/Highlands border replaced the Langford Speedway in 1955. British Columbia Automotive Sports Association officials and drivers assured full entries for the two-night opening in mid-May.

Owner Andy Cottyn, a logger and ardent racing fan, began clearing the land with a bulldozer in 1953, succeeding in spite of mud and snow to complete the track and grandstand in less than a year. His friend Jack Spalding helped line up cars and events for the opening. Interest in car racing continues to brings large crowds to the popular Langford track.

Andy Cottyn driving his logging truck, a re-built dump truck, into Langford at Suicide Hill south of the Goldstream Flats. (Cottyn family photos)

12
THE MALAHAT DRIVE

Langford extends part way up the Malahat Drive. This spectacularly scenic road dates from 1911 when it replaced an old wagon road that meandered over the mountain inland from the present highway to Mill Bay.

Narrow road, steep drop, no railings: two cars pass carefully at the Malahat summit shortly after construction was completed in 1911 on the road that follows Major MacFarlane's route.
(BC Archives E-00422)

The inland route was a major inconvenience for Cowichan Valley settlers who relied on a weekly steamer from Victoria for supplies, when the land route took as much as four days. They agitated for years for a more direct route, but bureaucrats in the Department of Lands and Works insisted that a more direct route along the Saanich Arm side of the mountain was an impossible dream.

However, the Cowichan Valley settlers persuaded a reluctant civil servant, Stanhope Farwell, to examine a proposed route along the west shore of the Saanich Inlet in 1874. Mr. Farwell's report dated June 3, 1874, describes his two-day expedition over the mountains to Victoria.

" ... I left Cowichan on the morning of the 25th [of May] accompanied by Mr. W. C. Duncan to examine the line blazed last October

...I started at 7 a.m. and reached Victoria at 11 p.m. having experienced very rough weather – snow, hail and rain the greater part of the day."

...the "innumerable turns and twists, and the steep grade to the Goldstream flat where it joins the Cowichan trail and runs along it near the side of the Goldstream House."

by Mr. John Nicholson for the proposed road from Saywards Mill [Mill Bay] to Goldstream … On Tuesday the 26th I started at 7 a.m. and reached Victoria at 11 p.m. having experienced very rough weather – snow, hail and rain the greater part of the day."

The first section of the route followed a lower bench near the west shore of the Saanich Arm for about three miles, then rose to an altitude of 382 feet back of the Malahat Indian village, about three quarters of a mile from the salt water. "Thence the line rises rapidly over a shoulder of the Mallahatt [sic] Mountain and attains an altitude of 1309 feet at some distance from the water." After several miles of rocky ground and detours along a creek to find a crossing, he began the southward descent.

"Thence to Goldstream the line is very crooked meandering round rocks and bluff. … The descent from the Goldstream Hill to the Flat is very steep and long. The line follows down the bank of a gully, through thick second growth fir and hemlock, a considerable distance and then follows round the hill till it reaches the flat. There are a number of steep inclines I did not measure, considering the [numerous grade measurements] sufficient to prove the character of the country." He estimated the entire distance at about 19 miles, twelve miles at an altitude varying from 643 to 1336 feet, "much of it over broken ground, loose rock and boulders, and in a great many places bed rock is visible."

His detailed description of the route included the "innumerable turns and twists, and the steep grade to the Goldstream flat where it joins the Cowichan trail and runs along it near the side of the Goldstream House." The gully and parts of the old road are now part of the trail system in the Goldstream Provincial Park campsite.

Stanhope Farwell sent his meticulous field notes to the Commissioner of Lands and Forests, but added an unfavourable opinion. "From what I could gather from hunters and others acquainted with the neighbourhood it might be possible to build a road near the line of the Cowichan trail, but there must be a steep rise from Goldstream flat to the top of the Mountain. In the event of a wagon road being constructed from Victoria to Cowichan I am satisfied there would never be a pound of freight hauled over it. A few people might ride over it and farmers might drive stock over it occasionally. … The settlers that I conversed with on the subject in Cowichan district generally considered the whole affair a waste of money," preferring

"… The settlers that I conversed with on the subject in Cowichan district generally considered the whole affair a waste of money,"

construction of a road to Nanaimo where the development of the coal mines would prove to be the settlers' principal market.

A report in The Daily Colonist of August 27, 1875, suggests that Farwell the civil servant "was not as physically agile as his guide, Mr. Duncan, so found the really steep climbs beyond his limited ability."

Two years later, F. G. Vernon, then commissioner of Lands and Works, heard from another staff surveyor sent to explore the route along the west shore of Saanich Inlet. A. R. Howse reported that "the surface of the mountain side is principally rocky slide, bed rock and boulders with patches of gravel at intervals." He added that the nearer he approached Goldstream the greater the difficulties he encountered: "steeper grades, rock slides and bed rock being the chief features.

"I am of the opinion that this line is quite impracticable for a wagon road, and moreover I am convinced that no suitable line can be found east of the Goldstream and Mallahat [sic] Range of mountains. I have the honor to be Sir Your most obedient Servant, A. R. Howse.

"I am of the opinion that this line is quite impracticable for a wagon road, and moreover I am convinced that no suitable line can be found..."

Part of the Malahat Drive showing the early route twisting up the hill from Goldstream Flats. Automobile owners added their demands for a passable route for their touring cars, unreliable vehicles that could never negotiate the old inland road. (View Royal Archives, Pearce Collection)

Howse also explored and recommended the route on the western side of the mountain range from Sooke Lake to Shawnigan Lake, which was more or less the route of the wagon road completed in 1884 and the Esquimalt and Nanaimo Railway line in 1886.

Wagons struggled up the old road for another 30 years before anyone made a serious attempt to survey the shorter route along the west side of the inlet. Major J. F. MacFarlane, formerly of the Royal

The first automobile made it over the mountain on June 3, 1911, according to notes on this photograph by William Penman.
(Victoria City Archives PR19, #32)

Artillery serving in India, was highly motivated to find an easier, shorter route from his 100-acre farm at Cobble Hill near Shawnigan Lake. He began his one-man survey in 1903 working through the wooded, mountainous country with hand compass and aneroid barometer, sometimes traveling the E&N Railway tracks on a borrowed handcar. He mapped out a route road over the mountains to the Goldstream lowlands, but Victoria officialdom was as uninterested as ever in his meticulous survey - until a provincial election loomed.

Major MacFarlane collected hundreds of signatures and took his ten-foot long petition to the legislature. Politicians hopeful of re-election jogged the bureaucrats into action. Two independent surveyors were sent to check the route and were astonished at the Major's accomplishment, completed on his own with his team of horses and a borrowed railway handcart.

The gravel road, following much the same route as the present much improved Malahat Drive, was completed in 1911, a considerable accomplishment at the time. Major MacFarlane is believed to have been the first to drive over it from Mill Bay to Victoria with his team of horses.

Driving the hazardous new road was not to be taken lightly in the early years. Preparations included checking spare tire, container of water for overheated radiator, rations for children in case of breakdowns. Hazel Olson described Malahat driving in the early days:

"The Malahat was certainly the supreme driving test. It was narrow and crooked, with steep hills and precarious corners. There were patches of gravel that had not been mixed thoroughly with dirt, and it became necessary to open throttles wide ... to plow through.

Broken axles, steaming radiators, burned out motors and flat tires were commonplace on this single-lane highway with no railings to protect or reassure drivers. Hairpin curves and the occasional rock or mud slide added to the intriguing journey. Failing brakes or poor judgment caused many accidents and occasional deaths."

In the spring of 1918 Axel Olson paid $400 for an "almost new" automobile, which impressed his bride-to-be immensely. Hazel wrote this description of the McLaughlin-Buick, which seems to have passed the Malahat test:

"[It had] heavy brass headlights and parking lights, operated with a combination of carbide and water, after lighting with a match. They gave off a foul odour but actually projected a fairly good light. Radiator, bracing rods, door handles were also brass. Solid heavy rubber tires cushioned a few of the bumps. Upholstery was of finest genuine heavy black leather. The car was black while the top, which could be folded down at the rear of the back seat, was of black canvas with isinglass windows when the top was up. Axel washed and polished the brass fittings regularly, showing off and transporting young friends to dances."

After World War II the road was improved to safer highway driving standards. The scenic route has been paved and widened, and motorists traveling over the hill north of Goldstream Flats no longer worry about overheated engines. Guard rails at the summit are reassuring. The view over the Saanich Arm is spectacular.

Improvements to a narrow stretch of the Island Highway at Langford Lake in 1938. This section of the road, now the western end of Goldstream Avenue, joins the Trans Canada at an intersection just north of the 1938 upgrade. (BC Archives D-07446)

New Langford, 150 Years Later

It's getting really hard to find traces of Old Langford in the booming new town that is about to become officially the City of Langford.

Captain Langford's home fell apart a century ago. The scenic Royal Colwood Golf Club occupies much of the land where his livestock grazed. A row of second growth evergreens along Goldstream Avenue is all that is left of the forest that surrounded his family home and the workmen's houses.

The general stores that sold groceries and feed have been replaced by suburban shopping malls and enormous 'big box' stores selling everything. These and the Western Speedway are the big attractions now for city folk traveling to Langford.

The modest little houses on their 10-acre farms have mostly disappeared, replaced since the 1950s by the architecture of the universal suburb. Recent developments north of the Trans Canada Highway lead the way with up-market homes, at prices formerly seen only in more affluent parts of the capital city of British Columbia.

Langford has been called many things in the past: The Gateway to the Malahat, The Land of the Chicken Ranches, The Egg Capital of British Columbia, and any number of really disparaging epithets. Even now the majority of townspeople know only what they see as they speed along the four-lane Trans Canada Highway or Veterans Memorial Parkway en route to or from somewhere else.

To see something of the olden days of forest and farms when the Parkway was still Millstream Road, drive the highway to Sooke Lake Road, up the hill to Ma Miller's pub (The Goldstream Inn). Turn left on Humpback Road until suburbia gives way to forest and a few farms in the shadow of Mount Wells. The winding road still follows the route of an old trail to Langford's southern border at Dewdney Flats on Sooke Road.

Pockets of farmland still exist along Happy Valley Road, between Sooke Road and the Metchosin boundary, but the lavender and herb farm and a tree farm have replaced poultry farms and sawmills. The back roads lead to undeveloped land, some still farmed.

To hike and picnic where early residents enjoyed their outings, try to find Atkins Road behind the new Western Communities RCMP building and a franchise restaurant. This will take you to Mill Hill Park, a steep climb to the top where the fire lookout used to be, but a quiet and pleasant walk beside a reasonably undisturbed section of historic Millstream.

Goldstream flats across the highway from the camp grounds is part of the Provincial Park where Victorians have marveled at the size of the giant cedars in the rainforest for over a century. There is no longer a tea room, but there are picnic tables and easy trails for a family outing. Watching the salmon come to spawn in the fall is another favourite thing to do. Mount Finlayson, now part of the park, is a stiff hike from the flats. (A parking fee was recently introduced.)

Public walkways around the three lakes are easily accessible for walks rather than hikes, and still have views once enjoyed from the hunting lodges and summer cottages of an earlier era.

We hope this story of times past will help explain why so many Old Langfordians would never want to live anywhere else.

Appendix I

LANGFORD AND THE HUDSON'S BAY COMPANY

Fort Victoria owed its existence to American westward migration, especially after the California gold rush in 1849. The Hudson's Bay Company traded everywhere west of the Rocky Mountains, from its northern forts in the Columbia District (now British Columbia) south to San Francisco. Their major fur trade establishment was thriving in beautiful fertile country around Fort Vancouver near the mouth of the Columbia River. To the annoyance of the HBC directors in London, international politics involving American and British territorial claims forced the Company to move its western district headquarters north to Vancouver Island. Oregon and the Washington Territory became part of the United States, and the American Government encouraged settlement by offering a land at a good price – free.

The British Colonial Office realized it would have to strengthen the British presence by increasing the population on its side of the 49th parallel. They declared Vancouver Island a colony and leased it to the Hudson's Bay Company in 1849 for seven shillings a year. One of the conditions of this arrangement was that the Company would make every effort to bring settlers to the colony. Their first efforts were half-hearted, fur traders being reluctant to encourage settlers into their lucrative territory.

By 1850 land on the British side of the boundary at £5 an acre was not attracting private citizens. The Company set up its four large farms and began promoting the opportunities on its rental island. It recruited farm managers, workmen and their families, and recorded them as settlers rather than HBC employees, thus fulfilling in their own way the conditions of their lease. (Only one officially independent settler, Captain Walter Colquhoun Grant, was persuaded to emigrate. He arrived in 1849, sold his unsuccessful farm at Sooke to coal miner John Muir, and left for home in 1853.)

The Puget Sound Agricultural Company was a creature of the Hudson's Bay Company, owned and managed by HBC directors. Under its umbrella the Company established four large farms west of the Fort, engaged three British bailiffs (the fourth, at Macaulay Point, was managed badly by a Hudson's Bay Company employee already at hand) as lords of the manors. As employees, they were accountable to the HBC directors in London who ignored warnings that most of the reserved land was unsuitable for agriculture as they knew it, and issued foolish orders anyway. The English gentleman's country estates promised in Company promotions never quite lived up to expectations.

Note: The reference to first settlers refers of course to European immigrants who arrived long after the Coast Salish Indians fished and hunted in the area. Their story should be told by members of their nation. However, it is worth noting that Langford's inland location was a less favoured site for camps and villages than those with access to the sea.

Dr. Grant Keddie, curator, archaeology, at the Royal British Columbia Museum, writes of the early Indian settlements in the western communities: There are many archaeological sites along the shoreline of Colwood. These include cultural deposits called shell middens, and in some cases, associated burial rock cleft and cairn burial sites. The shell middens represent the remains of both long term village sites and season campsites. The few that have been dated (at present) fit into the time period of the last thousand years. The animal bones from theses sites show that a wide variety of fish and bird species were utilized, as well as seals, sea lions, elk, deer and smaller amounts of land mammals such as raccoon and bear. There are small stone tool assemblages that have been found at inland localities. These would have been used for both mammal hunting and gathering of plant resources. Trout and Salmon would have been caught on a few of the streams. First Peoples would have crossed Colwood to gather the rich waterfowl resources on Langford Lake (there were no fish in Langford Lake based on early historic accounts.) (Correspondence with author, 2002)

Members of the Malahat and other families still have fishing rights in Saanich Inlet and the Goldstream River, and artifacts have been found on Mill Hill, indicating the presence of First People hunters on the mountains near the inlet.

Appendix II

INSIDE CAPTAIN LANGFORD'S HOUSE

"This house, into which the family moved in 1892, consisted of nine rooms, plus two more at the rear that were in such a state of disrepair as to be considered unsafe for occupancy. They were demolished at once. (*Ed. Note: Hazel speculates that the rooms were not part of the original house, but were added "presumably to accommodate a school-master or governess for Captain Langford's family." More likely this addition was built for Miss Louisa Langford's Academy for Young Ladies in the 1850s.*)

"A very rough sketch shows the layout of the original home. Some details of the construction and ornamentation both inside and out-side this spacious residence before its demolition have come to my attention. There were three bedrooms, a huge master bedroom with three windows, the others with two each, all made of tiny panes of glass. Windows were brought from England and considered a luxury fit only for those who could indulge in such comforts. The large dining room had two windows, the kitchen one, and a storeroom and pantry each contained one window. Four brick chimneys served two rooms each, and each contained deep fireplaces about four feet wide. One bedroom contained an additional outlet for a stovepipe.

"The kitchen was equipped with iron plates on which pots could be placed over the fire, and a large grate and crane made up this luxury equipment.

"The large ballroom [sic] had elaborately decorated upright supports for the mantelpiece, while all others were plain. Flanking the huge fireplace on either side were two shields, carved with a cross and the Roman Numeral X in the centre. I remember the shield well, red being the predominant colour, with the balance in brown and blue hues. As Aunt Daid [Daisy Wale] vividly recalls, deeply worn indentations in the wood above the shields would indicate that the heel of a heavy boot had rested there many times. Apparently some-one sat in front of the fire, tilted the chair backwards, placing his heels on top of the shields while he sat smoking or toasting his legs beside the open fire. As a child Aunt Daid regarded these imprints as an intriguing mystery ... Her contention was that the shields likely contained the family crests of Edward Langford

"Inside doors, which were painted, were of plain paneled wood. In order to keep the doors clean and also add ornamentation, there were small flat pieces of porcelain surrounding the doorknobs, some of which were yellow, others black and very shiny. Outside doors, made of thick heavy hardwood, were fitted with massive brass locks requiring a key about twelve inches long. The main entrance did not face the front, but instead opened onto a closed-in porch to the right of the veranda that extended the full length of the building nearest the road.

"The only inner door of any special significance was a rather spectacular one leading to the rooms at the rear, through a short hallway. This door, of varnished or oiled yellowish wood, possibly yellow cedar, had a huge steel coil spring, so stiff it was scarcely possible for a child to push open and squeeze through without being knocked down. As it thundered shut behind … it was almost impossible to avoid a violent slap on the backside …

"Thick plank flooring, squared on each side by hand with a broad axe, was smoothed on the upper side. The ballroom floor left much to be desired at the time the Wales moved in and shortly afterwards William installed a new floor over the old one.

"Outer walls were of thick plaster, much like stucco today. The closed in porch at the entrance contained two small windows, one on each side, while the front veranda had four small window panels in the upper half of double doors that swung outward on hinges, top and bottom, similar to Dutch doors. All floors were carpeted with the exception of the kitchen which was bare. A horsehair parlour suite furnished the room in which William and Ann Wale shared their breakfast. Plastered walls, about two and a half inches thick on each side, were well preserved, in a good state of repair, covered by rough two-by-four studding and hand-split cedar lath."

Appendix III

THE THREE KETTLES

Langford's three small lakes are within the Colwood Delta area, a gravel plain encompassing most of Langford and parts of Colwood and Metchosin. It was formed when streams from melting glacial ice ground up rocks on their way to the ocean about 13,000 years ago. As the meltwater in the Goldstream watershed flowed to the ocean or the Saanich Inlet it spread sand, clay and gravel over large parts of the western communities.

The lakes are the result of enormous blocks of stagnant ice which remained frozen long enough to gouge deep depressions in the otherwise flat delta. When these mammoth chunks melted like huge snowmen in the spring, the water remained. The lakes are still small independent bodies of water, neither fed by rivers nor draining into streams but relying on rainwater and surface runoff to refill and renew themselves. Langford Lake, for instance, refreshes itself slowly, approximately every three years.

The course of the meltwater streams could be seen until recently from Glen Lake across Jacklin road where it dips south of Station Road. But shopping malls, roads and parking lots now cover large parts of the ancient meltwater channels on their way to Colwood Creek, Colwood Golf course and Colwood Corners. (Colwood Lake has a shorter history: it was just a pond at the fourth tee of the golf course until it was excavated in 1957.)

When the E. & N. Railway trestle across the south side of Langford Lake was filled in, the railbed dammed the ebb and flow of water from the wetlands to the south west. Properties around the lake flooded. Some time around 1900 farmers in on the west side shoveled out a ditch to drain the wetland into the Goldstream River. The line of the man-made creek is shown as a ditch on some maps, as a tributary of the river on others. Hon. C. E. Pooley, who kept pheasants for hunting on the land he bought from James Phair, is said to have been one of the ditch proponents.

Langford Lake is also notable for serious problems resulting from residential developments, agricultural chemicals, gravel extraction, and further development proposed for the ecologically fragile land surrounding the lake. Foreign weeds and invading catfish gave the lake a few bad years. A lot of volunteer work by residents and a weeding machine bought at their own expense successfully cleared the foul weed. The Langford Lake Area Protection Society is still guardian of the lake. An aerator is activated each spring, by the Ministry of Lands, Air and Water, to mix layers of water during the summer. Lake water is tested regularly by Ministry staff working from a portable pontoon raft, an unusual craft which helps to keep fish thriving in Langford and other lakes in need of help.

The lake has been stocked every year by the provincial Land, Air and Water Ministry with rainbow trout since 1976 and coastal cutthroat since 1988. At present (2002) the lake receives 6000 catchable rainbow trout 4 times a year and 2000 yearling cutthroat trout from Vancouver Island hatcheries once a year.

Appendix IV

THE GOLDSTREAM WATERSHED SYSTEM

"For over 100 years the watershed lands, commonly referred to as the Sooke and Goldstream Watersheds, have been subject to a wide range of land uses: mining, transportation and utility corridors, commercial fishing, hydro power generation ranching, settlement and logging" (Capital Regional District Water Department)

In 1892 engineers began building dams and tunnels connecting lakes and streams along the Goldstream River to supply water to Victoria. Natural lakes and wetlands were converted to controlled reservoirs, some of which still serve as backup storage during drought, maintenance or emergencies.

The Goldstream dams were built between 1892 and 1914 and upgraded in 1995 to meet seismic standards. The Goldstream River system, still the second largest in the area, consists of three small lakes, Butchart, Lubbe and Japan Gulch Reservoirs, several channels and the Kapoor tunnel. The number of lakes and wetlands within the Goldstream and Sooke watersheds has been altered by the construction of dams, first for power generation in 1898 and later for the city's domestic water supply. Natural channels have also been modified to divert water to the system and to protect water quality from streambank erosion.

Water for the Humpback reservoir, the earliest but no longer in use, came from two other reservoirs to Waugh Creek. The screening tower and lower dam are still there.

The entire watershed at the western boundary of Langford is now closed to the public except for guided tours.

Acknowledgements

Thanks first to two people who have worked tirelessly for the past four years to ensure that Langford finally has a record of its early history: Allan LeQuesne who saw the need for a book about Langford based on memories of long-time residents, and Lisa Francis who volunteered to assist with research. Allan's knowledge of the area as a native son and fire chief for 33 years gave access to many of the old Langford families. Lisa's research involved many interviews and hours of internet research, as well as her diligent search for old photographs. Her organization of masses of material and sources contributed greatly to putting this history together.

Special thanks to Arthur McTavish for lending his copy of the two-volume history of the pioneer Scafe and Wale families, a treasury of Langford stories compiled by his aunt, Hazel Scafe Olson, and edited by her son Almer. Thanks also to John Oliver and Bonnie Josephson for sharing their knowledge of Happy Valley history; to Alec Merriman for information about Langford Lake; Dawn Cropp for facilitating access to the Goldstream Museum during its transition period; to Margaret Roper for providing access to the Metchosin School Museum photographic collections, and to Bob Adamek and the Greater Victoria Water District for a tour of the restricted area of the Goldstream Watershed. We also appreciate help from members of the Langford Fire Department who kindly arranged for use of old photographs from their archives, and from Langford municipal mapping technician Sean Elliott.

Assistance from staff of several British Columbia archives has been much appreciated, especially from David Mattison and Kelly Nolin at the Provincial Archives, Carey Pallister at the City of Victoria Archives, Trevor Smith of the Esquimalt Archives, Louise Baur of the View Royal Community Archives, and others contacted by phone or e-mail. The Greater Victoria Public Library reference department and libraries of Provincial ministries have also helped to find useful documents.

My editor Lynn Gough, who read through early and late drafts, deserves special recognition for zeroing in on problems and wisely suggesting solutions. Thanks for this and all the encouragement during the process. And to Alan Murray for finding things all the rest of us missed.

The long list of Langford residents who spoke to us at coffee shop interviews and by telephone, or sent information by mail and e-mail, includes Laurie Rhode, Verna (Rhode) Langrish, Ken Langrish, Jean Strachan, John Oliver, Ben Swindell, Jim Jackson, Alan Bodman, Tom Thorpe, Dick Rant (since deceased), Eric Clay, Maria Forsland, Jim Isaacson, Kathleen Hooney, Dorothy Newcomb, Gordon and Lillian Cooper, Roy Tennent, Derek Orchard, George Cottyn, Ruth Pearce, Myrna Harling (since deceased), Ken and Bunty Hincks, Rod Bayles (since deceased), Garry Lockridge, Sid Finch, Fred and Jim Chidlow, Barb Carlow, Wallace Klages, Darryl Muralt, Bernie Nichols, Norm Wilcox, Ross Rocket, Lillian Price, Marie Fisher, Alan Robertson, Ian McKenzie, Norma Lohbrunner, Albert Jacobson, Dorothy Hobbis, Barrie Goodwin, Alice (Linton) Hayes, Jack Payne (since deceased), Eileen (Turner) Smith, Rosemary (Bullen) Brimacombe, Linda Hogg, Valerie Braunschweig, Jack and Ritchie LeQuesne, Adela (Yates) Abel, Mary (Rockingham) Hughes, Alison Gardner and Val Hughes, Roberta (Basustow) Jones, Godfrey Stevens, Bunty Frewing, Dewane Hala, Loren and Nancy Fuller, Ken Cameron, Dave Munro, Sandy West, Kelly Zado, Ken Caffery, Claude and Sheila Bugslag, Mr. and Mrs. Gene Valcourt and many others who suggested further contacts. We have tried to check the stories, but recollections differ. Some of the more recent stories could not be used in this history of earlier days but will be valuable for future researchers. A word of thanks also to Gordon and Lorraine Maxwell, Lyle Kahl for use of his office for several interviews, Westside Instaprint and Brantek Packaging for photocopying.

Apologies for any errors that may have crept in between interviews and publication – and many thanks for the memories.

Sources

Unpublished papers, theses and club histories:

Meyers, Thomas Rathwell: 90 years of Public Utility Service on Vancouver Island. Typescript, 1959. Victoria.

Baker, F.W, and Mrs. Baker. The Bakers Round. Shanghai. Self published, 1932. (Private Collection)

Coyle, Brian C. The Puget's Sound Agricultural Company on Vancouver Island, 1847-1857. Vancouver. Master's thesis, Simon Fraser University, 1977.

Neumann, Natasha. Geology and History of Mining at Goldstream. 1991 for Geological Association of Canada, Pacific Section., 1991. Energy and Mines Ministry library No. 557.1134 N492

Klages, Wallace. Book of Remembrance. Langford. 1999.

Littler, Alan. Metchosin Farmers' Institute. 1996.

South Vancouver Island Rangers. Anniversary booklets, 1972, 1987.

Newspapers:

The British Colonist, The Daily Colonist

The Evening Express (Victoria)

Victoria Gazette

Goldstream News Gazette and its predecessors, including the Juan de Fuca News

Archives and Libraries

National Archives of Canada

Provincial Archives of British Columbia

Hudson's Bay Company Archives, University of Manitoba

City of Victoria Archives

City of Vancouver Archives

Anglican Diocese of British Columbia Archives

Goldstream Museum

Metchosin School Museum

Nicola Valley Museum/Archives Association

Esquimalt Archives

View Royal Archives

Greater Victoria Public Library, local history reference department

BC Ministry of Mines library

Victoria and British Columbia directories

Published Sources:

Adams, John. Old Square Toes and His Lady – The Life of James and Amelia Douglas. Victoria. Horsdal & Shubart, 2001

Akrigg, C.P.V. and Helen B. Akrigg. 1001 British Columbia Place Names. Vancouver, 1970.

Crocker, Liz. A Cultural History of Three Regional Parks. Victoria. Capital Regional District Parks, 1999.

Douglas, Jill, Ed. Modern Pioneers. British Columbia Women's Institute, Evergreen Printing, 1958. Victoria.

Duffus, Maureen. A Most Unusual Colony: Vancouver Island, 1849-1860. Victoria. Desktop Publishing Ltd., 1996

————Craigflower Country – A History of View Royal, 1850-1950. Victoria. View Royal Historical Committee, 1993.

Fawcett, Edgar. Some Reminiscences of Old Victoria. Toronto. William Briggs, 1912.

Gough, Barry M. The Royal Navy and the Northwest Coast of North America, 1810, 1914. Vancouver. UBC Press, 1971.

Helgesen, Marion I., ed. Footprints – Pioneer Families of the Metchosin District, Southern Vancouver Island, 1851-1900. Victoria. Metchosin School Museum, 1983.

Jones, Ron. End of Eden, Reminiscences of a Forest Ranger. Summerland, BC. T. L. Publishers, 1989.

Lugrin, N. deBertrand. Pioneer Women of Vancouver Island, 1843-1866. Victoria. The Women's Canadian Club of Victoria, 1928.

MacLachlan, Donald F. The Esquimalt & Nanaimo Railway – The Dunsmuir Years: 1884-1905. B.C. Railway Historical Association, Victoria. 1986.

Pettit, S.G. The Trials and Tribulations of Edward Edwards Langford. Victoria: B.C. Historical Quarterly, XVII. pp5-40, 1953.

Phillips, Geraldine. High Heels to Gumboots. Victoria. PR Books, 2001

Pritchard, Allan, ed. The Vancouver Letters of Edmund Hope Verney. Vancouver. UBC Press, 1996.

Stranix, Dorothy. Notes and Quotes. Victoria. Joint Centennial Committee for Colwood, Langford, Metchosin, Happy Valley-Glen Lake. nd.

Smith, Dorothy Blakey, ed. The Reminiscences of Dr. John Sebastian Helmcken. Vancouver. UBC Press 1975.

Walker, Doreen, ED. Dear Nan, Letters of Emily Carr, Nan Cheney and Humphrey Toms. Vancouver. UBC Press, 1990.

Yorath, C.J., and H. W. Nasmith. The Geology of Southern Vancouver Island: A field guide. Victoria. Orca Book Publishers, 1995.

————Victoria Illustrated. Victoria. Ellis & Co., "The Colonist," 1891

————Picturesque Victoria. Victoria. T.N. Hibben, ca. 1900.

Websites:

District of Langford

Langford Lake Area Protection Society

Flewin Family website

Capital Regional District

Open Door website

B.C. Archives Visual and Textual records

U.K. Census and Vital Statistics records

Index